1

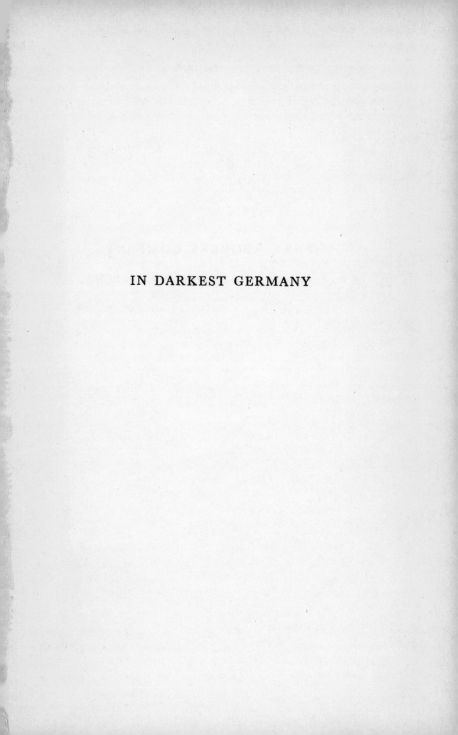

IN DARKEST GERMANY

HENRY REGNERY COMPANY

The Devin-Adair Co., 23 E. 26th St., New York 10, N.Y.

DISTRIBUTORS

IN DARKEST GERMANY

BY

VICTOR GOLLANCZ

WITH AN INTRODUCTION BY ROBERT M. HUTCHINS

"Are ye not as children of the Ethiopians unto
me, O children of Israel? saith the Lord.
Have not I brought up Israel out of the land
of Egypt? and the Philistines from Caphtor,
and the Syrians from Kir?"   AMOS, ix. 7

HINSDALE, ILLINOIS

HENRY REGNERY COMPANY

1947

FOR

ERWIN STADTHAGEN

INTRODUCTION

THIS IS A remarkable book. In a time when the individual has been lost in the mass and when ideals are regarded largely as a means to mislead and deceive, we have, in Victor Gollancz, a man who can still think and speak of human beings, rather than of Germans, Jews or Russians, and to whom the ideals of our Christian heritage are sacred.

The picture of misery and despair which this book reflects is based on first-hand information gathered during October and November, 1946. It is unfortunately necessary to report that conditions one year later will probably be little better, and may even be worse. Although the Directives issued July 15th, 1947, to General Clay represent at their face value a complete change of policy from that prescribed in the Directives of May, 1945, they may prove to be equally futile and unworkable. Orders, even if issued from the highest levels, provide in themselves no guarantee that they will have the desired effect, and while Washington now wisely gives the Germans the right to find their own form of democracy, there are still many conditions attached to their freedom of action.

General Clay is told that we are seeking a "loose federal government for Germany." What constitutes in the eyes of Washington and General Clay a too-centralized form of government? Would the Weimar Republic, for example, be regarded as such a government? This, certainly, involves the exercise of a kind of "external" political influence which we ourselves have denounced in principle.

These new Directives assume the maintenance of a paternalistic military rule in Germany, regardless of what may be said about permitting the Germans to live according to "democratic principles." The principles of self-government and of liberty for the individual are difficult to realize under external supervision, no matter how benevolent or well-intentioned. The new Directives, although a welcome step in the right direction, do not alter the basic character of the military occupation.

Such alterations as have been made in detail and in ultimate purpose will, let us hope, give the Germans some improvement of their physical situation. They do not, however, create the atmosphere in which work prospers. We have allowed Germany to sink into a state of despair and misery and in doing so have threatened the structure of the entire continent. We now desire to halt the downward decline. We grant some concessions. For the moment they may appear impressive. But we should not delude ourselves into thinking that Europe is saved. In Germany we shall demonstrate to the world whether our ideals of freedom, individual rights, and democracy have any real content.

This book—written by a man who is a Socialist and a Jew—is one of the first to attack the barbaric policy of the victors toward the vanquished on the basis of the Christian ideal. It is not strange that Victor Gollancz should write such a book, but it is a reflection on the times in which we live that his is almost the only book which has approached this problem on the basis of the one real issue involved in it—namely, moral values.

ROBERT M. HUTCHINS
July 1947

THANKS

I WISH TO express my gratitude to Norfolk House, for the facilities afforded to me and the arrangements so kindly made for my comfort and convenience; to Brigadier Treadwell, General Fanshaw, Air Vice-marshal Champion de Crespigny, Mr. Griffin, Mr. Harry Walston, and Brigadier Bonsey for their gracious hospitality; to Public Relations in the zone, and particularly to Mr. Nicol, Mr. Tom Guthrie, and Major Scott-Atkinson; to my conducting officer, Peter Flynn, my devoted driver, Mr. Singer, and my superb and indefatigable Hamburg photographer, Herr Beutner, as well as to the excellent photographers at Düsseldorf; to Mr. Hickey, who interpreted so brilliantly at Düsseldorf; to Mr. Berry, Regional Commissioner for Hamburg, Mr. Lumley, Regional Economic Officer in that city, Brigadiers John Cowley and Michael Robinson of Minden, and Herr Petersen, Herr Landahl, and Dr. Degkwitz of Hamburg and Landesrat Meier of Düsseldorf for very special courtesies; and to all the officials, British and German, who bore so patiently with my wearisome questionings, as well as to the many German citizens who received me with unvarying courtesy when I ventured to enter their dwellings and to ask them about their circumstances.

No one here mentioned must be assumed to agree with any of the views I express.

V. G.

CONTENTS

FOREWORD

I LEFT LONDON for the British zone of Germany on October 2nd and arrived back on November 15th. This is, I believe, the longest visit paid to the zone since victory. Two or three weeks have usually been considered more than adequate, and Mr. Hynd, the Chancellor of the Duchy, said the other day in the House that during the last twelve months he had spent no more than twenty-eight days in Germany. I mention the length of my visit only to excuse myself for my temerity in publishing a book, or rather an apology for a book, about my findings. The time proved, in point of fact, quite insufficient for the purpose I had in view; and when I thought it necessary to hurry back home there was a great number of matters the mere fringes of which I had been unable to investigate. I could not even penetrate to Berlin.

But what I did examine during those six or seven weeks I examined with care. Though I visited other places as well, such as Bünde, Herford, Minden and Kiel, I spent most of the time in Hamburg, Düsseldorf and the Ruhr. I tried my best to master subjects of which I previously knew nothing, and this often involved a lengthy cross-examination of British and German officials, the checking of one against another, and sometimes the re-examination of both. I may well have been betrayed into some errors by my ignorance; but unless in what follows I qualify any statement by "I think", the reader may assume that every alleged fact has been checked, whenever possible, to the best of my ability. I adopted the attitude of a sceptic to everything I was told, whether by British or by Germans.

When I got back, I had to decide how best to make use

of such knowledge as I had been able to acquire. In view of what I felt to be the deplorable situation in the zone speed seemed essential, and to sit down and write a carefully planned book quite out of the question. I decided therefore to write immediately for the Press as many letters and articles as possible on different aspects of the problem, and simultaneously to present some sort of report to those Ministers, Members of Parliament and responsible people generally to whom I might be able to gain access. In all some eighteen letters or articles were published within a fortnight or so of my return.

But I was repeatedly asked to publish something which, ephemeral though it in any case must be, might at any rate be more convenient to handle than a mere series of newspaper cuttings. I was again faced with the problem of time, particularly at a moment when the delays in book production are unconscionable. I thought the best thing, therefore, would be to bring together the stuff I had already written, cut out the obvious repetitions, and add a good deal of supplementary information. That is how this βιβλιον ἀβιβλιον has come into being: and I apologize for its odd shape and its lack of literary graces.

The same feeling of urgency has prevented me from dealing with many important subjects. I should have liked, for instance, to write of our information service, which I gathered to be deplorable both in big things and in small. I was told, for instance, by an official of very high regional rank that when the rations were cut in March there was a lapse of many days before any serious explanation was given: and that no real attempt was made to "put over", to use his phrase, the recent increase in taxation and cut in pensions. I report this statement with reserve, for I had no opportunity of checking its accuracy. But in general several of the most intelligent officials complained to me that "things were constantly being done without reason given". Of the same order was what was described as quite a series of broken pledges. It was alleged that issues both of tea and of extra tobacco were promised but never materialized. The disastrous muddle in the matter of domestic fuel and of Sunday work by the miners was primarily due to an inaccurate Press release, which infuriated the miners and convinced their leaders that they had been "let down".

The supply of information to our own people is equally inadequate. I can state, this time with no reserve at all, that one of the most important zonal officials first heard something crucially affecting his department when he read of it in a London newspaper during a few days' leave: and I was informed by more than one responsible member of the Control Commission that they "got a lot of valuable information that vitally concerned them from *The Times*". I had personal experience of the intellectual starvation not only of the Germans but of the British too. At a headquarters mess at which I stayed for more than a fortnight you never knew what paper might be turning up: one day it would be *The Times*, on another the *Daily Express*, on a third the *Daily Mirror*. At another mess you were bare of information if you were out for lunch, for people used to disappear to their bedrooms with newspapers concealed about their persons. I was told that whenever I personally did this I looked extremely guilty. My conducting officer spent quite a large portion of his time stealing newspapers for me from different messes: he even achieved the triumph of stealing one from my own.

I should also have liked to write about the general decline of public morality under the impact of the growing despair and of a financial chaos in which the black and grey sectors constantly encroach on the legitimate one, and the mark becomes more and more meaningless. Technically illegal transactions are, indeed, so open that the epithet black is a misnomer. A business man wants something he can't get legally: he tells his secretary, and an hour later

15

he has it. Girls packing seeds abscond with a few packets, and make as much as the head of the firm. A charwoman has only to "pinch" a sack of coal in order to earn the equivalent of at least three months' wages. The result is that the youth is growing up with no idea of morality at all. A technical school in Hamburg is one of the black market centres for that city. "What does the teacher say?" one of the pupils was asked. "He's glad if every now and again he gets something out of it himself" was the reply.

Most important of all the omitted topics are those of youth work and education generally. The total establishment of our youth section, of which it is impossible to speak too highly, is, or was when I was there, twenty-three. I have the record of a conversation with an official familiar with the work of this section. He said that paper, equipment and premises were virtually unobtainable. In June two thousand Nissen huts had been promised: the number had been reduced in July to five hundred: by October none had been delivered. In July one per cent. of the bid for timber and point one per cent. of that for steel had been received, for repairs to cover all educational necessities. In our zone there was only one youth magazine, a monthly: in the U.S. zone there were nine, mostly fortnightly. Denazification had made the work almost impossible, as ex-regular officers could not be used as leaders. The amnesty for youth was, at that time, hanging fire: and there had been the utmost difficulty in sending a few representatives of the new German youth, as they should be sent, out of the zone. On the regional level, I was informed in North Rhine–Westphalia that there were no books, magazines, handicraft materials, indoor games, or outdoor sports equipment for youth work, and no special allocation of fuel for meeting places. This is the general picture; and while of course the difficulty of priorities must always be kept in mind, my impression was that youth work was very near the bottom of them, whereas it ought to be not far from the top.

If the reader finds in the text nothing about these questions, or that of elementary, secondary and university education, this is certainly not because I underestimate their importance.

. . . . .

Any section that has already appeared in the Press is suitably labelled, and I take this opportunity of thanking *The Times*, *The Times Literary Supplement*, *The Manchester Guardian*, *The Observer*, *The News Chronicle*, *The Daily Herald* and *The New Statesman* for permission to reprint. It does not follow that the original is reproduced exactly: I have cut out, added and combined. But in no case have I found it necessary to correct either a fact or an expression of opinion as the result of anything that has been written or said since my return to England.

I would add that all the photographs were taken in my presence, except where I have stated to the contrary on the reproductions. I must beg pardon for the intrusion into some of them of my body, hand or even face. I thought that my visible presence would add verisimilitude, and obviate the charge, for instance, that these were really agency photographs taken in China in the year 1932.

. . . . .

It will be appreciated that I have written throughout of the position as I found it in October and early November. The future is governed partly by that position, and partly by the Anglo-American fusion arrangements which have just been announced, and which must build on the existing situation. Clearly some of the evils that I attempt to describe will be remedied, if only partially, by these arrangements. The question is, how many and how partially? *The New Statesman* has rightly said that acceptance or rejection was a choice of evils, but has wrongly, in my view, concluded that there is more to be said against than for. I think, on the contrary, that there is more to be said for than against—but only just. Clearly, the disastrous raw materials position will be to a certain extent remedied: there will be some sort of import–export programme: and financial reform is at least mentioned, albeit quite barely and without even a hint of the kind of plan to be adopted—probably because no such plan yet exists. All this is to the good; but there is a great deal that is very bad indeed. I deal with the question of food in the text. Hardly less and perhaps in the long run even more important, the plan appears to be based on the March "level of industry", which would be disastrous in a unified and intact Reich, but is sheer lunacy in the Anglo-American trunk for which we are admittedly legislating. To judge from the proposed credits, the import programme will be far too meagre to allow of real recovery, given the appalling position at present existing. Moreover, Anglo-American co-operation will bring its own special problems. Mr. Bevin and Mr. Dalton insist that the nationalization of key industries in the British zone is not in any way prejudiced, but it seems to me clear that American influence will be all in the other direction, and good intentions will be hard put to it if they are to get the better of American intransigence. Again, the same American influence will strengthen reactionary tendencies towards a disastrous economic particularism in the *Länder*, and, more generally, will encourage the stupid federalism which must beat itself in vain against the logic of history. A federal Europe, a hundred times yes: an atomized Germany in an unfederalized Europe, danger and folly.

And, fusion or no fusion, a great deal of the present trouble can be remedied by ourselves alone, and only by radical changes both in the spirit with which we approach our task and in the method and machinery of administration. Here we have conspicuously failed. This is not intended as a criticism of Mr. Hynd, who is named more than once in the following pages, but only because, being the Minister responsible, he must inevitably bear the weight of attack. There is no humaner man in British public life, and no one whose attitude to the German problem has been, not merely since the end of the war but long before it, more consistently generous and sensible: but a man of these qualities, even if of supreme ability, could achieve little without a revolution in policy far above his head.

    .   .   .   .   .

I want to add a few words which may appear personal, but are in fact written in the name of all those, at first very few but now a rapidly growing number, who have been trying, some for as long as eighteen months, to bring to the public attention the facts about Germany. We have been charged with preferring enemies to friends, ignoring the sufferings of the Indians, the Chinese, the Greeks, the Poles or the Yugoslavs, and generally behaving like irresponsible featherheads. We repudiate this charge, which is ridiculous. I personally was chairman of the China Campaign Committee from the mid-thirties to towards the end of the war, founded with Eleanor Rathbone the National Committee for Rescue from Nazi Terror in 1942, and in the years before the war published a whole series of books and made many hundreds of speeches about the abominable rapes of Austria and Czechoslovakia and about fascist wickedness in Spain. If we have had to concentrate the major part of our energy on Germany during the last eighteen months, that is not because we believe that Germans are more important than anyone else: it is because we believe that they are not less important, and because they had few, and at first very few, to appeal in their name to the decency of the world. We further felt that as nationals of an occupying Power that had enforced unconditional surrender we had a very special responsibility before the bars of history and of our own consciences; and we reflected that, if every German was indeed responsible for what happened at Belsen, then we, as members of a democratic country and not of a fascist one with no free Press or parliament, were responsible individually as well as collectively for refusing to tolerate anything that might be considered even remotely comparable with Belsen, if only by way of rhetoric. There was the further fact that, in the matter of food, Unrra was doing at least something for other countries, but nothing at all for Germany, where in the absence of any government of her own effective aid could come only from those allied countries which, by a deliberate act of policy, had stripped her of great food-producing territories.

I have written this, as I say, in the name of my colleagues in "Save Europe Now", of a growing band of Members of Parliament, and of the few exceptional newspaper correspondents, such as those of *The Times* and *The Manchester Guardian*, who for so many months have been waging an unceasing fight for decency and justice. But when it comes to it I must add something that really is personal. As most people are aware who are aware of me at all, I am a Jew: and I am sometimes asked why, as a Jew, I bother about people in whose name infamies have been committed against my race, the memory of which, I fear—though I would wish it otherwise—may never die. I am sometimes asked this, I regret to say, by fellow-Jews who have forgotten, if they ever knew, the teaching of our prophets. It has also been suggested that in my work for the Germans I am, in some deliberate and offensively self-conscious sense, heaping "coals of fire". I wouldn't much mind if this were true, for what matters is not a man's motive but any practical result that may follow from his work—and in the present case that, I am sorry to say, has so far been distressingly small. The charge, however, is untrue and ludicrous. It is indeed a fact that I feel called upon to help suffering Germans precisely because I am a Jew: but not at all for the reason imagined. It is a question neither of "coals of fire" nor of what is called, and so often miscalled, sentimentality. It is a question rather of plain, straight commonsense, undeflected by that very sentimentality which deflects the judgment and corrupts the spirit of so many. To me three propositions seem self-evident. The first is that nothing can save the world but a general act of repentance in place of the present self-righteous insistence on the wickedness of others; for we have all sinned, and continue to sin most horribly. The second is that good treatment and not bad treatment makes men good. And the third is—to drop into the hideous collective language which is now so much the mode—that unless you treat a man well when he has treated you ill you just get nowhere, or rather you give further impetus to evil and head straight for human annihilation. People talk, or used to talk, of the mission of Israel. This mission, if it exists, is not to blow up people in Palestine; our mission is, just because we have been specially insulted and outraged for 1,900 years or more, to be specially ready for reconciliation. I say this in no spirit of criticism of those, whether they be Jews or Frenchmen or Czechs or Poles, whose sons or wives or lovers have suffered such agony and shame that even now one dare not think of it, and who can therefore neither forget nor forgive. I understand very well the thoughts and feelings that are their daily portion. But just because this awful legacy of hatred is, for our poor humanity, all but inevitable, so much the more incumbent is it upon those of us who have suffered only vicariously, if at all, to balance their bitterness by our well-wishing.

Once or twice, in Germany, I found that it was more than well-wishing. In what follows the reader will find, as a description of what I felt in Jülich, the word "affection". I thought it significant that the article in which the word occurs was rejected by the two papers to which I offered it, whereas everything else was immediately accepted. I wondered whether I had better cut the word right out, and also the epithet "dear" which occurs in a letter from Hamburg. But then I remembered that I was trying to give a truthful account not only of what I saw but also of what I felt: and I reflected that most of the objectors, if they had been with me on the spot, would have found what I found— namely that, in the hearts of those who have been so fortunate as to remain unembittered by the tragedy of life, the presence of suffering evokes a kind of love. So I decided to print and be damned.

V. G.

14 Henrietta Street,
   Dec. 13th, 1946.

IN DARKEST GERMANY

I

FOOD AND HEALTH

§ (i)

BRITAIN AND DÜSSELDORF

To the Editor of The Times.

Sir,—Here in this ruined city, where we as conquerors are presumably responsible for at any rate the bare necessities of the population, it is impossible to read Mr. Strachey's Dundee speech on the food position in England without an almost unbearable sense of shame. Even after rationing, says the Minister, we are eating a little more flour as bread and cakes than before the war, 98 per cent. as much meat, and nearly 50 per cent. more fish.

Though, say, 80 per cent. of the town population in our zone of Germany supplements the official ration by a few hundred calories—through the black market, which is keeping people alive, or from other sources—the condition of millions is indescribably wretched. One expert whose job it is to make an assessment of such things estimates that in the city of Hamburg some 100,000 people are suffering from hunger œdema or the equivalent; and according to figures given to me by the German public health authorities 13,000 people in Regierungsbezirk Düsseldorf were being treated for this illness in hospitals or by private practitioners during the month of September. I saw at a hospital in Hamburg a starving man who had been brought in a few hours before: his death-rattle was beginning. I had a photograph of him taken—with me by his side, to save myself from the charge of exaggeration. I saw another man in the same hospital whose swollen scrotum reached a third of the way to the floor. I have a photograph of him also.*

I have just returned from visiting a "bunker"—a huge air-raid shelter, without daylight or air, where 800 children get their schooling (Plates 1–3). In one class of 41 children, 23 had had no breakfast, and nothing whatever to eat until half-past two, when they had had the school meal of half a litre of soup, without bread. Exceptionally it was pea soup to-day; it is usually "biscuit soup". Seven of these children had the ugly skin-blemishes that are mixed up in some way with malnutrition; all were white and pasty. Their gaping "shoes"—these, too, have been photographed—mean the end of what little health they have when the wet weather comes.

Particularly horrible is the growth of tuberculosis. It is difficult to arrive at exact figures owing to imperfect systems of notification in some places. But in Hamburg it is certain that active lung tuberculosis is at least five times as prevalent as before the war, and it may even be ten times as prevalent. The number of active cases registered in that city at the end of 1944 was 9,886; at the end of 1945, 12,013; and on July 1st 1946, 16,808. As only cases in hospitals and dispensaries are registered, these figures indicate the appalling growth of the disease, but not, of course, the real total of suffering persons.

There are two main reasons for this increase in tuberculosis—malnutrition and overcrowding. In the British zone 12,000 people with open, infectious tuberculosis live in the same room with others—sometimes in the same bed

* I have decided at the last minute, after a great deal of hesitation, to suppress the photographs of these two cases, except that of the second man's face (Plate 4). I have similarly suppressed all other photographs of really bad cases of œdema where the water is still present, as I cannot bear to perpetuate a visible record of these horrors. (In hunger œdema the body swells, sometimes abominably, with water.) I have retained a photograph of a less terrible case of emaciation, and one or two of œdema where the water has gone.

with children. I shall make no attempt to describe housing conditions—your readers would not believe me. But I shall show my photographs when I return to England.

Apart from better housing, it is, above all, more meat that is required if an increasingly rapid growth of tuberculosis is to be prevented. Must we eat 98 per cent. of the meat we ate in England before the war, when we are at the same time eating more bread and nearly 50 per cent. more fish? Even a very small cut would make such a difference to the 23,000,000 Germans in our charge. And I am told by experts that if we make the "sacrifice", the amount so saved could come to the Germans—there would be no difficulty with the International Emergency Food Council.

The people in the cellars and bunkers of ruined Germany, and particularly the women and children, are for the most part wonderfully brave, and "break down" only when they are given a bar of chocolate, or whatever it may be, by a shamefaced visitor. If Mr. Attlee would only come out here and see for himself, it is inconceivable that he would maintain the ban on private food parcels.

Yours, &c.,
VICTOR GOLLANCZ.

Düsseldorf, Oct. 30.

§ (ii)

HUNGER ŒDEMA

[My letter to *The Times* of October 30th produced a reply from some distinguished Unrra consultants. They challenged my figures, not explicitly but by implication, but seemed most concerned to emphasise the claims of Unrra countries.]

To the Editor of The Times.

Sir,—No one could have more sympathy than I with the motive of Dr. Meiklejohn and his colleagues, which is, I am sure, not to minimize the plight of the Germans but to avert disaster from eastern Europe, now so gravely menaced by the disgraceful decision to close down Unrra. While, however, the motive is admirable, the method seems to me less satisfactory. Figures are quoted with no apparent understanding of their nature and meaning. During the six weeks of my visit to the British zone, on the other hand, I have laboriously checked and checked again every fact and figure given to me both by British and German authorities, and have refrained from putting pen to paper until I have satisfied myself that I have correctly appreciated the position. On the question of tuberculosis, for instance, I have spent many days "digging down" and attempting to discover what may be the truth underlying the many conflicting views presented to me. My statement that "active lung tuberculosis in Hamburg is at least five times as prevalent as before the war" is, I am persuaded, correct.

Space will permit me to deal with only one point in detail—namely, that of hunger œdema. "Certainly the situation [in Hamburg] must have deteriorated in a most alarming fashion since the end of July," write your correspondents, "when the Control Commission reported 1,189 cases of hunger œdema in the city." But these were hospitalized cases. You must first add the non-hospitalized cases; and the relation of the one figure to the other, which no doubt varies from place to place, may be gauged from the fact that in certain districts of the North Rhine province, for the period from July 1 to October 19, there were 48 known but non-hospitalized cases for every one hospitalized case. And when you have done that you must further add the cases that come to no one's attention, but can be estimated from surveys.

It is not a question of old ladies with varicose veins. I have personally seen only two women with hunger œdema, though I have seen many who are painfully emaciated. Some indication of the true position is provided by a survey recently made (under British auspices) of the nutritional state of about 1,000 employees of the *Reichspost Direktion*, Hamburg. In males of all ages the incidence of hunger œdema was found to be no less than 17 per cent., and in females of all ages 9 per cent. These are horrifying figures. "This is a clinical assessment," says the report, "in which there was always a higher incidence among persons examined in the afternoons, and this regardless of whether or not theirs was a sedentary job. The incidence of this cardinal sign of malnutrition must therefore be even higher in fact. Further, it should be borne in mind that among large numbers of persons in the same general state of under-nourishment necessitating hospitalization little more than half do manifest this sign." It was to the latter fact that I referred when I wrote "hunger œdema or its equivalent". No less than 52 per cent. of the males and 34 per cent. of the females in the same group showed "marked loss of flesh", and 24 per cent. of the males and 22 per cent. of the females "looked positively ill".

Finally, your correspondents question the figure of 13,000 officially given by German public health authorities as the number of people in Regierungsbezirk Düsseldorf being treated for hunger œdema in hospitals or privately during September. This scepticism is not shared, apparently, by responsible British officials on the spot. "Recent surveys by Public Health in the Regierungsbezirk Düsseldorf," reported the Colonel commanding R.B. Düsseldorf to the Deputy Regional Commissioner in June, "showed that the number of hospitalized cases of people suffering from hunger œdema was comparatively low, the reason being shortage of beds. The number of non-hospitalized cases is high—in the region of 25,000."

Allow me to add a word in conclusion. The most horrible of my experiences has been a visit to the camp at Belsen, where I saw the tattoo marks on the arms of the

Jewish survivors. I am never likely to forget the unspeakable wickedness of which the Nazis were guilty. But when
I see the swollen bodies and living skeletons in hospitals
here and elsewhere; when I look at the miserable "shoes"
of boys and girls in the schools, and find that they have
come to their lessons without even a dry piece of bread for
breakfast; when I go down into a one-roomed cellar where
a mother is struggling, and struggling very bravely, to do
her best for a husband and four or five children—then I
think, not of Germans, but of men and women. I am sure
I should have the same feelings if I were in Greece or
Poland. But I happen to be in Germany, and write of
what I see here.

Yours, &c.,
VICTOR GOLLANCZ.

Düsseldorf, Nov. 12.

§ (iii)

TURKEYS AND STARVATION

To the Editor of The News Chronicle.

Sir,—The shamelessness of the Government becomes in-
tolerable. Turkeys and poultry specially imported, extra
meat, sweets and sugar—these are among the luxuries
which Mr. Strachey announces for Christmas. I don't
know what sort of part my friend Strachey has played in
making this monstrous decision; if any part at all, he is not
the Strachey I worked with for so many years.

Have these Christian statesmen of ours the slightest idea
of what is going on in Germany? Apparently not, for if
they had they would not make the idiotic statements that
cause such consternation among intelligent members of
the Control Commission. Let me tell them, then, something about life here in this ruined city of Düsseldorf.

The normal consumer's ration is supposed to be one of

1,550 calories a day—about half ours in England. But this week four of the items that account for most of this bogus figure—bread, cereals, skim milk, and even vegetables—are either non-existent or in horribly short supply; and the same has been the case, in varying degree, ever since I've been here.

The bread famine has meant that after standing in the queue hour after hour and day after day since six o'clock in the morning—and it is now vilely cold—many have been turned away empty handed. In Wuppertal there was no bread at all for 10 days.

The plain fact is that that portion of the Düsseldorf population that cannot, or will not, supplement the ration by a few hundred extra calories from the black market or other sources—the old, the feeble, the lonely, the very poor, the hardest working and the over-conscientious—have been living these last days on anything from 400 to 1,000 calories. Four hundred—and I have been in many homes where this has been the daily ration—is half the Belsen figure.

I wish Mr. Attlee, Lord Pakenham—whose speech in the Lords was a model of feebleness and futility—and Mr. Strachey could have been with me a couple of days ago in the big hospital here, when I spent a ghastly morning photographing cases of hunger œdema and emaciation. I cannot believe that they would not have been as sickened as I was.

Our prestige here is pretty near the nadir. The youth is being poisoned and renazified. We have all but lost the peace—and I fear that this is an understatement.

Yours, &c.,
VICTOR GOLLANCZ.

Düsseldorf, November 8.

A REPLY TO MR. STRACHEY

[A reply by Mr. Strachey was published in *The News Chronicle* the day after the above letter appeared. Next day Mr. Cummings commented.]

To the Editor of The News Chronicle.

Sir,—A. J. Cummings says that "it is absurd, as well as grossly unfair, to suggest that the British Government is indifferent to elementary human needs in the British Zone". It is not absurd; it is not unfair; it is the fact. Listen to this.

Private food parcels—to be made up from rationed foods only, spared from his own ration by the would-be donor—would be invaluable.

I don't want anybody to tell me that they would hardly touch the fringe of the problem; after six weeks in Germany I know all about that a good deal better than many of the objectors. But, first, every individual case is an individual case, and if one person out of every hundred or ten thousand can be spared extreme hunger, then that is so much gain; and, secondly, it is impossible to exaggerate what such gestures mean in giving evidence of human solidarity.

American parcels are now beginning to arrive in our zone, and I have personal experience of what they mean to the recipients. That the Americans are sending parcels and we are not will be still another count against us; and this will be doubly lamentable in view of the fact that the American all-over failure is indeed far greater than ours.

Now what has happened about these food parcels? The following. "Save Europe Now" had been attempting for months to get them sanctioned; and when Strachey replaced Ben Smith at the Ministry of Food it seemed certain that the scheme would go through.

We worked out the details with officials of the Ministry

and the many other departments concerned at a number of extremely tedious conferences.

Then the whole thing collapsed. Why? Because bread rationing was introduced, and the Government, alarmed by an outcry which was very largely as bogus and engineered as it was in any event disgraceful, simply refused to face the hypothetical charge that "in so grave a domestic crisis" it was allowing food to go out of the country— idiotic though such a charge would be, since every bit of the food in question would simply be transferred from an individual and willing consumer in England to an individual consumer in Germany.

I challenge both Attlee and Strachey to deny that this is a true statement of the facts; and I say that this is just one example of indifference—or, if you like, comparative indifference—to elementary human needs in the British zone.

I see that Hynd has now made another of his famous "optimistic" speeches. It will send a cold shiver down the back of every intelligent member of the Control Commission—as in the case of his recent Berlin effort, on the very eve of the present appalling crisis in the Ruhr. Everyone in Germany is asking: "Where on earth does Hynd get his information from?"

. . . . .

As for John Strachey, he is so intelligent, and his reply so feeble, that I must assume that he has got himself mixed up with a policy of which he disapproves, and is making the best of it.

What Germany must have, he says sagely, is not turkeys or sweets, but regular cereals. He's telling me! But

(*a*) He misses the point that to give us extra Christmas rations, over and above the high general standard of living of which he talked with so much pride recently, is morally degrading to ourselves and must add still further to the growing cynicism with which the Germans regard "Western democracy";

(*b*) The Germans need, God knows, the "variety" of which Ben Smith had always a deal to say; and they might have had a little of it, but for our selfishness, this Christmas;

(*c*) They desperately need animal proteins. I believe I am right in saying (but will not vouch for it, as I am away from my documents) that if the Germans of our zone had been given the amount of meat by which our ration was recently increased, they would thereby have received a regular additional 50 per cent.* And now we take still more meat, as well as specially imported turkeys and poultry; this extra Christmas ration of meat alone would suffice to give four pounds to every child in the British zone. The fact that the miserable German fish ration has been quietly reduced for the current period makes matters worse;

(*d*) "You can't feed 'Germany' on sweets." How true! But if Strachey had been with me when a Salvation Army man gave sweets to some children in a miserable underground cellar where they "live" he might have grasped the point.

The Cabinet, says Strachey, knows exactly what is happening in Germany. No doubt; but usually after it has happened. How otherwise explain, among other things, Hynd's Berlin speech?

Yours, &c.,
VICTOR GOLLANCZ.

14, Henrietta Street, November 16.

§ (v)

A REPLY TO MR. HYND

To the Editor of The Times.

Sir,—In the debate on Wednesday (November 27th) Mr. Hynd, speaking about food in Germany, said: "I do

---

* The figure should be 70 per cent.

not think there is any difference between Mr. Gollancz and myself." There is a world of difference.

"The calculations upon which my statements are based," he continued, "are those of the actual amount of food that has been distributed. . . . We have maintained the ration steadily up to the present time, apart from local breakdowns." This is untrue.

On arriving in the Ruhr (October 27) I visited homes and schools, and was horrified by what I found. Many were living, the day I visited them, on a cup of milkless "coffee" for breakfast, potatoes with cabbage for lunch, and the same in the evening, bread being entirely absent.

I then made official, but still local, inquiries. I first discovered that the 1,550 calories were, even officially, a myth. The ration is made up of 14 items: there is a printed sheet showing the quantity of each item and the calorie value of that quantity, and these calorie values add up to 1,548. But while the public is entitled to the printed quantities in the case of 12 of the items, they are not so entitled in the case of bread and cereals. In the case of these two, the Press announces each week how much may be bought. The amounts shown on the sheet as necessary to make up the 1,550 calories are 10,000 grammes of bread and 1,750 grammes of cereals for the 28 days. But during the period which started on October 14—the period for which rations were officially raised to 1,550 calories—the amount of bread to which the public was entitled, even officially, was not 10,000 but 8,500 grammes; and the coupons for cereals were not "called up," in the official phrase, at all except in an infinitesimal percentage for special classes only. So the 1,548 calories have already become 1,206.

But it was clear to me that many were not getting 1,206 calories or anything like it. So on November 8 I went to Bonn and spent the day there with our Regional food team, which is responsible for North Rhine–Westphalia. I found a general impression that, though there had been breakdowns for a few days here and there, the thing had evened out and that over the whole period the 8,500 grammes of bread (but not, of course, the 10,000) were being met. I was unable to accept this assurance, and it was courteously agreed that certain towns should be rung up with a view to discovering in each case the stock of flour at the opening of the period, the amount necessary to meet the ration (on the 8,500, not the 10,000, basis) during the first three weeks of the period, the amount actually received during those three weeks, and the closing stock. When the results came through they showed a deficiency in Düsseldorf of about 50 per cent. and in Essen, Mülheim, Oberhausen, Duisburg, and Dinslaken, taken as a group, a deficiency of about 35 per cent. It was added that deliveries from small mills were not included, but that these would not seriously affect the general picture.

I then asked about cereals. The responsible officer stated that these had been unobtainable for a considerable period, that there was no possibility of an early resumption of supplies, and that the back-log would have to be written off.

I next inquired about skim milk. I was first told that 80 per cent. of the ration had been met. Again I could not agree, and begged for inquiries. The reply came through during the afternoon: over the whole North Rhine region the deficiency since October 14 had been about 50 per cent.

Mr. Hynd is the last man in the world to deceive the House of Commons. What, then, is the explanation?

Yours, &c., VICTOR GOLLANCZ.

14, Henrietta Street, Nov. 28.

RATIONS AND THE FUSION PLAN

To the Editor of the Manchester Guardian.

Sir,—Mr. Dalton, announcing in the House on December 3 the plan for the fusion of the British and American zones of Germany, said that "the food ration of 1,550 calories for the normal German consumer must be accepted for the present, but will be raised to 1,800 calories as soon as conditions of world supply permit." This statement will be read with the greatest disquiet. Several considerations arise:

1. "A diet containing an average of about 2,650 calories a day . . ." says the report of the Emergency Economic Committee for Europe, issued on February 6, 1946, "has been recommended by the U.N.R.R.A. Food Committee as the amount of food sufficient to maintain full health and efficiency in a population with a normal distribution according to sex, age, and occupation." A diet of 1,800 calories for the normal consumer seems, therefore, a curious target, even if it is not the ultimate one.

2. How long is the 1,550 scale to be retained? A week or so ago a well-known and reliable correspondent of the "Observer," writing from Berlin after an interview with responsible officials there, put the probable period at close on another year. This is folly. "A diet of 1,200 calories," according to the fourth report from the Select Committee on Estimates, House of Commons, November 5, 1946, "may be characterised as slow starvation . . . 1,550 calories is probably no better than even slower starvation." Moreover, the Germans had been living for many months on no more than 1,000 calories, and some of them, from time to time, on considerably less. Against such a background the prolonged continuance of 1,550 calories must inevitably involve a still more rapid deterioration in the

general health and in particular a progressively intensified increase of active lung tuberculosis.

3. What arrangements are being made to ensure that even the 1,550 calories will really be met? As everyone knows, they were far from being met during the period starting on October 14. For the following period, starting on November 11, a quota of cereals representing nearly 200 calories was put on the official sheet with a view to bringing the total up to 1,550. But I was assured at the Regional Food Headquarters in Bonn that these cereals would, in fact, be virtually unobtainable.* Maintenance of the ration will require a regular reserve of, at the very minimum, a month's supply of grain. Is this being provided for? When it comes to our own country Mr. Strachey considers a reserve of eight weeks the indispensable minimum. Unless we cease to work on a hand-to-mouth basis there will be constant repetitions of the disgraceful breakdown I witnessed in Düsseldorf and the Ruhr.

4. How is the diet to be composed? In the period starting October 14 the daily quota of visible fats for the normal German consumer amounted to 6 grammes (7 grammes = $\frac{1}{4}$ ounce), and that of protein to 43·1 grammes, 11·6 of which were animal protein. But I am informed by a leading expert that for building up bodily resistance 70 grammes of protein are essential, of which 30 should be animal protein, and that, while there is no definite

* The following answer by Mr. Hynd on December 11 is really almost unbelievable. The "current" period, as at December 11, is not the period starting November 11, which would be bad enough; it is the period subsequent to that. Here are the question and answer:

Mr. Foot asked the Chancellor of the Duchy of Lancaster what proportion of the cereal ration in North Rhine–Westphalia was met during the 28-day period beginning 14th October and is being met in the current period; and why has the cereal quota of the current ration been retained at 1,500 grammes. *Mr. J. Hynd:* Since 14th October only an insignificant proportion of the cereal ration, as distinct from bread, has been met in this region. I hope, however, that imports of grain will soon be sufficient to enable the full rate of distribution to be resumed and the ration scale has therefore been retained at 1,500 grammes.

evidence to prove that fats are necessary for health, it is, in fact, extremely difficult to "live" on less than 20 grammes of visible fats a day.

"This is the beginning of the end of our economic problems," said Mr. Bevin when announcing the plan. Unless its food arrangements are drastically revised his optimism will prove misguided.—Yours, &c.,

VICTOR GOLLANCZ.

14, Henrietta Street,
December 4.

§ (vii)
MORE FACTS ABOUT HEALTH

It is easy enough to get a reliable general picture of the state of what is called "public health" in Germany today. No one could doubt that it is deplorable, except the sort of person who concludes that nothing can be wrong if he doesn't see every second person dropping dead before his eyes. But it is difficult to get accurate details. Opinions vary a good deal about statistics and their meaning. Some, but by no means all, of the British doctors (who come largely, one gathers, from the R.A.M.C. and I.M.S., and a few of whom seem naturally predisposed to regard every sick man as a malingerer) are suspicious of, or even downright hostile to, their German confrères; and some, but by no means all, of the German doctors tend to exaggerate—which is certainly a fault in the better direction. Within a few days of my arrival I had a remarkable interview with a British medical officer of fair importance. He started by advising me always to see English doctors; he was so emphatic on the point that I realized at once how important it was for me to see German doctors as well. He agreed that "there wasn't enough penicillin", but his own explanation—"the Germans can't pay for it"—appeared, in his view, to dispose of the matter once and for all. I was to remember what he said when I saw a man a few days later at the University Hospital of Hamburg, in agony because there was no penicillin for him—you can see his face for yourselves on plate 5. This doctor also suggested that the German authorities had falsified the V.D. figures—penicillin at that time being permitted only for cases of gonorrhœa—"to get more penicillin". As to insulin, hospitals, he said, had 100 per cent. of their requirements—"and bad cases presumably go to hospital". I was to remember this too, when I was told by a German doctor whom I learned to trust that people forced their way into hospitals when the coma was about to come on in order to compel admittance. I next learned that all the people suffering from œdema, for instance in the Hamburg hospitals, were oldish—and so they might really be suffering from other kinds of œdema, such as cardiac or renal. So indeed this one or that one might; but the general impression that the remark might have conveyed to the unwary would have been wholly false, as I shall presently show. I ended the interview by asking whether any drugs etc. were in seriously short supply, and if so what, and in what order of priority. I got a satisfactorily categorical answer—penicillin, insulin, liver extract, cod-liver oil and malt, vitamins A and D.

.　　.　　.　　.　　.

In Kiel I found a high proportion of the people with grey and yellow faces, and I shall have something to say about this later on. Here, also, I was to have my first experience of a characteristic in the population that literally forces itself more and more on your attention: people drift about with such lassitude that you are always in danger of running them down if you happen to be in a car—as, being a Britisher, you almost invariably are.

On the day after my arrival in this city I went into the tuberculosis figures for Schleswig-Holstein. Tuberculosis is one of the things about which you have the greatest difficulty in arriving at the truth, as I was soon to discover.

There are many reasons; in Hamburg, for instance, until a few weeks ago only open infectious cases were notified and, as I mentioned in *The Times*, only cases in sanatoria and hospitals were registered. The number of notified and registered cases, therefore, is an imperfect guide to the amount of active tuberculosis, even by way of comparison with 1939, as general conditions are now so much worse, and in particular such hordes of "expellees" have been flooding into our zone and so many doctors have been "denazified" that there is likely to be a considerable percentage of tuberculosis that never comes under notice at all. Some attempts have been made here and there to get an all-over picture by mass X-ray surveys of the population; but these have to be treated with great caution, first because the samples are small, and secondly because a proportion of the "conspicuous pulmonary findings" certainly indicate bronchitis, old healed cases, cases in process of cure, etc. Nevertheless, these surveys must be taken into account.

The number of new cases of active lung tuberculosis registered in Schleswig-Holstein during the first six months of 1946 was between four and five times the number of new cases registered in the whole of 1939, and more than five-sixths of the number registered in the whole of 1945. The population is now double what it was in 1939. The registered figures for 1946, therefore, show something between a four-fold and a five-fold increase over 1939, after correcting the population statistics. After a similar correction, deaths from the disease during the first six months of 1946 come out as more numerous than those for the whole of 1939. I think I am right in adding that the monthly figures this year were rising steeply up till August, with a small drop in September; and that the number of new cases registered in that month was more than 60 per cent. higher than the numbers registered in January and February respectively.

As to the real increase since 1939, a layman's guess is as good as a doctor's, once he has had the whole thing explained to him. My guess is that for Schleswig-Holstein the increase is at least ten-fold, and probably far more. The horde of "expellees" is one of the reasons, of course, for the particularly bad situation in this *Land*.

Infant mortality in Schleswig-Holstein for the first six months of 1946 was at the rate of 116·1 per 1,000 live births, against the 1936 figure (for the Reich as a whole) of 66. But in the zone generally infant mortality is at the moment declining: it was 136 per 1,000 live births in January 1946 against 61 in January 1938, but only 75 (provisional figure) in August 1946 against 57 in August 1938. It is to be hoped that the winter will not see another rapid increase.

An interesting report has been written by Dr. Walter Büngeler, Dean of the Faculty of Medicine at Kiel University, about general health conditions in Schleswig-Holstein:

"The pathology of the post-war period is controlled by the direct or indirect results of deficiency- and undernourishment, which are becoming increasingly evident amongst the majority of the German population. Among cases we have investigated death through starvation has occurred only twice. Apart from this the effects of undernourishment have been established by the fact that all dead persons, even those who have died as a result of an accident or some acute infection, have been appallingly underweight. A 30% weight deficiency is by no means uncommon. Especially in the spring and summer of 1946 an enormous loss of substance in the vital organs was most striking in a large number of post-mortems. A 50% loss of weight in the liver and heart was frequently noticed. Finally already in middle age osteoporosis has been clearly established. . . .

"In the summer months of '46 the indirect results of deficient- and under-nourishment became far more evident. To this category belongs also the increased virulence of tuberculosis, with comparatively high mortality, which has been proved in our clinics. In almost all TB cases we find unusually disproportionate weight and frequently symptoms which prove a loss of immunity far exceeding the usual proportions (galloping consumption, unusual symptoms of generalisations of TB in adults).

"Furthermore septic infections frequently show unusual symptoms. Serious infections appear after relatively harmless staphylomykosis of the skin and flesh. Also the individual symptoms which then appear show emphatically the completely inadequate powers of resistance of the body.

"This general lowering of immunity leads also to loss of immunity and resistance in those organs whose physiological task it is to protect the body, and which now only show localised resistance in the form of inflammation, instead of general resistance.

"In this connection must be mentioned the extraordinary frequency, seriousness and persistence of skin staphylomykosis since this winter. External hygienic conditions have aggravated this tendency. The mucous membrane of the stomach and intestinal canal is normally a barrier to germs. Genuine intestinal infections have, however, not been so common as a result of appropriate hygienic measures. Almost all typhoid cases observed by us follow an extraordinary course. Clinical observations confirm these findings. Various relapses have been noticed, and even in serious typhoid cases, which later led to death, the level of the agglutinations-titre remained abnormally low or non-existent.

"All these observations explain to us the nature of an intestinal infection which up to now was most rare, but which has recently been increasing: acute or sub-acute unspecified enteritis phlegmonosa.

"This disease was up till now so rare that every case was given publicity. Up till 1923 forty cases were known in Germany, in more recent times there were known in Germany a few notifications. At the end of spring 1946 cases begin to appear again and they have meanwhile reached alarming numbers. . . ."

.　　　.　　　.　　　.　　　.

From Kiel I went to Hamburg. One of my early visits there was to an elementary school for girls, the age group being 6 to 14. I saw three girls being medically examined. The first had an underweight of 7 pounds, the second of 8, and the third of 17, but my arrival had been expected and these may perhaps have been specially selected cases. I was told that there was a regular underweight in the school of 8 pounds, and that there had been a great deterioration since the ration cut in March; but I had no means of checking this statement. The girl with the 17 pounds underweight was very small for her age, and pot-bellied. It was at this school that I first saw the horrible skin blemishes which I was later to see in all the schools I visited. The headmistress told me that 50 per cent. of her children suffered from them, and from counts I personally made elsewhere I should say that this was not a very serious exaggeration. The complaint takes various forms: very small red marks over a large area of the body, sores of the impetigo type, and small flat carbuncles which half heal and then break out again. My own view is that dirt and lack of soap are the origin, but that immunity is reduced, the trouble aggravated and a cure prevented by malnutrition, and in particular by the lack of meat, cheese, milk and eggs.

I went on to an elementary school for boys, where I saw children chosen for a "recovery home". You will find a photograph of some of them on plates 6 and 7.

I have already given the Hamburg tuberculosis figures in my letters to *The Times*. I would only add that the figure of five times pre-war is, in my view, a very conservative one, and was arrived at after several very lengthy cross-examinations. Two supplementary figures are oi interest. The official British public health review for Hamburg, January to June 1946, states that 5,321 new cases of active TB were registered at clinics during these 6 months, against 5,818 for the whole previous year; and in one Hamburg hospital for children, out of 425 beds occupied in 1939 there were 20 cases of tuberculosis, whereas in the same hospital, with approximately the same number of beds, these cases now number 170. I was assured that this was a fair sample, and that it conveyed a terrible warning; for children catch tuberculosis far more easily than adults from living in the same room with the infectious. In general, the present overcrowding means a progressive infection—one person infects two or three others, and so it goes on. Owing to shortage of beds in sanatoria urgent cases cannot be taken in; and people who in normal times would be isolated in a room at home are now living and sleeping with three, five, eight others. Unless this process stops, no one can see the end. "About 4,000 cases of infectious tuberculosis", says the Hamburg report already referred to, "were being nursed in their own houses, and under the bad and overcrowded housing conditions constituted a serious menace." The reference is, of course, only to known cases.

There was an improvement in the infant mortality rate for Hamburg similar to that for Schleswig-Holstein. It was (approximately) 50 per 1,000 live births in 1938, 145 in 1945, 125 in January 1946, 77 in March 1946, 114 in April 1946, 82 in June 1946, and 84 in July 1946. Miscarriages, on the other hand, which according to statistics of the Hamburg Health Authority were 12·2 per cent. of reported pregnancies in 1940 and increased about 1 per cent. a year till the end of 1945, when they reached 17·7 per cent., jumped during the first six months of 1946 to 20·1 per cent. A gynæcologist, with a practice in middle-class and intellectual circles, attributed the increase to food shortage, insufficient clothing, lack of fuel, bad housing conditions, homes overcrowded with strangers, queuing up by the hour for food, inadequate transport facilities, and overcrowded trains. His report continues:

"All this results in general in a considerable lowering of women's power of resistance and energy, and in particular it affects the female generative organs.

"Otherwise thoroughly healthy young women and girls suffer to an alarming extent from hypoplasia uteri. This is partly the result of shocks received during air raids, partly caused by the unfavourable change in the mode of living and by the barely sufficient one-sided food. It is very alarming in so far as it is a bad prognostic for conception. The treatment is very much impaired by the lack of all hormone preparations and the impossibility to send the women to suitable convalescent homes. That is where help is urgently needed.

"Inflammatory diseases of the abdominal organs, especially chronic catarrhs of the vagina, inflammations of the bladder, and nephritis, have to be increasingly dealt with during consulting hours. In many cases they are the result of staying insufficiently clothed in unheated rooms. The rise in gonococcal infections is very serious.

"The wish to have a child is waning. Instead of desiring a child many women are now succumbing to a deep despondency, thus the diagnosis of a new pregnancy often arouses fits of despair. The women are weighed down by the anxiety how to procure the most necessary things for the expected baby. There are no beds, no bedding, no baby-clothes and diapers. On account of the bad housing conditions a confinement at

46

home is generally out of the question, and the maternity wards are overcrowded. . . .

"Abortions are on the increase. Admission and production of contraceptives are urgently required in the present times of distress in order to restrict to a minimum illegal interruptions of gravidity which are often very detrimental to the health of the women."

This specialist's reference to abortion is confirmed from other sources; in one city I was told "The doctors are living on abortion."

As to hunger œdema in Hamburg, there is little to add to what I have written in *The Times*. I am satisfied that the estimate of 100,000 is a reasonable one; and it must be remembered that the survey of post-office workers was carried out under expert British auspices, and that but for it the existence of the majority of such cases would probably never have been known. The survey makes nonsense, of course, of the "old people with renal and cardiac œdema" argument. When the reader looks at the photographs of cases of œdema and emaciation which I took in various hospitals,* he must bear in mind that doctors are sometimes in error, and that this case or that may in fact be due, for instance, to kidney trouble or cancer. But the point is that this is what bad cases of œdema and emaciation look like, and that a very high percentage of them are unquestionably caused by starvation. I will give further proof of this later on.

Fortnightly weighings of industrial workers have been undertaken in Hamburg. Though the report of the Welfare Committee responsible for them states that the figures are "average figures of such a great group of population that they give a true picture of the loss of weight" I quote the findings with all reserve, as I lacked the time to investigate the *expertise* of the body in question. The figures, as

* I have suppressed most of these. See p. 24.

at the end of June 1946, show an average loss varying, in different groups of men and women, from 8 per cent. to 15 per cent. The weighings of children show no loss of weight up to 5 years of age, and average losses in other groups varying from 3 to 10 per cent. Weighings in old people's homes show an average loss of 20 per cent. for both men and women.

·   ·   ·   ·   ·

On October 15 I paid a visit to the University Hospital of Hamburg, where I took photographs. A chart prepared by Professor Jorez showed that of males weighed on admittance in 1939, whatever their complaint, 25·7 per cent. were overweight, 15 per cent. more than 5 kilos underweight, and a further 12·8 per cent. more than 10 kilos (about a stone and a half) underweight. Similar weighings in June 1946 showed 1·8 per cent. overweight, 19·4 per cent. more than 5 kilos underweight, and a further 49·3 per cent. more than 10 kilos underweight. These figures may be considered reliable. The Professor also informed me that the weight of mentally deficient children at the Alsterdorf Anstalt was generally normal in 1939, but in the second quarter of 1946 was deficient in the case of girls by an average of 6 kilos and in the case of boys by an average of 9½ kilos (again, nearly a stone and a half); and that the mortality rate in this institution had increased from roughly 1 to roughly 5 per cent.

I enquired about the rations of hunger œdema patients. I was told that these, even for the worst cases, amounted to only 2,300 calories. I would remind the reader that in England the average calories are at the moment just on 3,000.

·   ·   ·   ·   ·

From Hamburg I went to Düsseldorf and the Ruhr. I will give first the public health figures for the North Rhine Province as given me in a document dated November 6th and prepared by the German M.O.H., Dr. Gerfeldt.

Population: October 1939, 6,500,000; September 1946, 5,947,000, including about 250,000 refugees. Active cases of tuberculosis on the register: 31st December 1944, 9,902; 31st December 1945, 19,102; 30th June 1946, 25,000. This information was supplemented verbally at a conference with Dr. Gerfeldt and other leading German public health officials. They stated that the real figure was probably about 33⅓ per cent. higher than the one shown; that 6,000 known cases of infectious tuberculosis were not isolated: and that at a clinic for all children's diseases in Stadtkreis Düsseldorf the number of cases of tuberculosis was about two and a half times as high on September 30th 1946 as on January 1st 1939. There was a similar rise in the death rate from children's tuberculosis in this institution.

At the same conference I was given body-weights in the North Rhine Province, as follows. Children from 6–12: in Düsseldorf (I think the Regierungsbezirk, but possibly the town only), normal 81·4%, middle (loss of weight less than 3%) 4·8%, bad (loss of weight more than 3%) 14%. In Cologne, normal 11·7%, middle 58·8%, bad 29·5%. In Regierungsbezirk Aachen, normal 9%, middle 23%, bad 68%. In the whole *Land* North Rhine–Westphalia, average underweight in men 8·5% and in women 7·5%.

The British public health authorities added the information that in North Rhine–Westphalia the total number of known infectious cases of tuberculosis at the end of June was 23,500, but the number of beds in hospitals and sanatoria only 10,066. They further stated that in North Rhine, while there had been little increase in new registered cases as between January and June 1946, there had been an increase of nearly 33⅓ per cent. in open and infectious cases during the same period. The Friends Relief Service have recently reported from Dortmund that in Landkreis Iserlohn nearly 33⅓ per cent. of all the children examined there were TB positive.

While in Düsseldorf I visited three ordinary schools, as well as the bunker school referred to in the *Times* correspondence. In a class of 45 boys aged 6 or 7, only one, I thought, looked healthy. Many were clearly under-nourished, and there was a plague of spots and sores. In another mixed class of children of 13 or so the under-nourishment of all the boys without exception was even more noticeable; most of the girls, on the other hand, looked fairly normal. Many of the boys had swollen glands. I had a few undressed. Photographs will be found on plates 14 and 15.

I spent November 2 at Oberhausen, a typical mining town. Mr. Buist, the *Times* correspondent, and I got away from the officials and entered miners' flats at random. In two tiny rooms we found a mother and father, a baby that looked as if it wouldn't live, and three other children. Two of the children were barefoot; the other had a pair of house-shoes borrowed from the man's father-in-law. By way of bedclothes there were 3 blankets for the whole family and nothing more. The miner had money, but no *Bezugsmarken;* he had done his best to get them but without success. It must be explained that you can't just go into a shop and try to buy a shoe or almost any other personal or household necessity; you have first to obtain a *Bezugsmark,* or coupon, which you may—but usually do not—receive on proof of need. If and when you have got it you then have to go from shop to shop—sometimes, recently, even from town to town—to try to get the article.

I suspected what these children would look like naked, and was horribly torn between shame at asking to photo-graph them and desire to bring conditions like this home to the British public. When I asked the mother's per-mission she broke down and was comforted with difficulty by Buist, who however eventually persuaded her that this might be a way to help Germany. You will find the photographs on plates 16 and 17.

Back in Düsseldorf, I spent a morning (November 5th) at the Town Hospital. I saw a few very badly underweight children there—the trouble was, the doctor said, that they had to be sent home without proper shoes and clothes, and so got ill again. I also saw a child of ten with heavy TB—the kind of TB, I was told, that you find normally only in babies. The disease was spread over the whole body, and bandages could be changed only under morphia. Such cases, it appeared, were today much commoner in older children. Previously there had not been enough to fill the building; now another building, as well as this, was full. Photograph on plate 18.

One of the patients at this hospital was its own lady doctor. She lived alone, was too busy to get food from the Black Market, and couldn't queue up; so she had had no bread for weeks. She was now recovering slowly from hunger œdema.

At the baby clinic attached to this hospital I was told that only one in three mothers could feed her baby properly; the breasts of the others were dry within a week.

Later in the day I had a talk with Dr. Arnold, the Burgomaster of Düsseldorf and one of the half dozen best Germans I met. During the last few weeks, he said, he had been visiting factories and workshops, and had personally examined people in Stadtkreis and Landkreis Düsseldorf, as well as in Essen, Bochum and the Ruhr generally. The condition of the men was so bad that their working capacity was on the verge of collapse. He had noticed that when miners and metal workers were bathing at a distance of 8 yards he could count their ribs. He had been told by factory doctors that within a period of three months there had been losses of 15 to 20 lbs.

Dr. Amelunxen, the Minister-President of North Rhine-Westphalia, spoke in a similar sense. He was convinced that during the next few years two or three million would die as a direct result of present conditions—old people, the tuberculous, and a very large number of young children who would fail to overcome the normal childish diseases. Many senior British officials are equally alarmed. "There is a general deterioration in the health of the population" wrote the Colonel commanding Regierungsbezirk Düsseldorf to the Deputy Regional Commissioner on June 25th "and in their ability to resist disease, which is having an adverse effect on their morale. There is a considerable increase in the number of cases of hunger œdema in the larger towns in the R.B., notably among women and old people and business men who are at work all day. Stillbirths are on the increase. . . . Simple ailments, such as colds, boils, carbuncles etc., which would normally be treated at home, have now to be treated in hospital, and complications often follow. People have been seen collapsing while waiting in queues, and for the Düsseldorf ferry." He proceeds to give some particulars from Essen, Wuppertal, Oberhausen, Solingen, Düsseldorf, Mülheim and Remscheid. "In Düsseldorf on 19th May there were 145 cases of hunger œdema in one hospital (Grafenberg). Of 934 persons reported to one of the Stadtkreis Medical Officers, 200 were found to be suffering from hunger œdema, and only 70 were in normal health." "In Mülheim average loss of weight in hospital 20%. Increase in number of hospital patients in one year 18% to 20%." "In Remscheid definitely undernourished in April 6,648, in May 7,259. Suffering from lack of albumen April 1,732, May 1,792." Then follows the estimate of 25,000 as the number of persons in the R.B. suffering from hunger œdema, which I quoted in my letter to *The Times*.

I thought I would round off the whole investigation by having a talk with a world-famous British expert on nutrition, who was doing special work in the neighbourhood on hunger œdema. He was as cautious as a scientist no doubt should be, and he had a poor opinion of the veracity of Germans in general and of German scientists in particular. Nevertheless, the upshot was substantially to confirm my own conclusions. He could not say whether the prevalence of spots and sores was due in some degree to malnutrition. He agreed that the majority of adults you saw about looked yellow (as well as thin); but the reason, he said, was not clear to him. If I understood him aright, he thought that the yellow, parchmenty appearance might be caused by a failure of the blood to flush the skin. "A sort of defence mechanism" suggested one of his assistants. But when I put a direct question, the answer was a frank "Of course, it's connected in some way with malnutrition". As to œdema, he explained, as so many others had explained already, that only some of it was hunger œdema, and that this type could easily be identified by its quick response to extra food. Later on in the conversation, when I was asking another question about œdema, "You'd be surprised" I was told "how many of the cases that pass through my hands improve very rapidly when quite a small amount of additional food is given." These cases, then, must have been hunger œdema.

All this doesn't mean, as I said at the beginning, that people are dropping dead in the streets. The crude mortality rate has been improving and in August was normal. The point is that a very great number of people feel wretchedly weak and ill, and that the health of the population as a whole is being undermined with such startling rapidity that, unless radical measures are taken to effect an improvement, the toll in one, two or three years' time will be appalling. It must be remembered that mortality from tuberculosis did not reach its climax until five years after the last war. Even the increasing prevalence of infectious diseases is not the most important aspect of the matter, serious though this is. In the Control Commission's information room at Bünde there is a chart headed "Diseases of the German Population", and showing a graph of seven diseases with March 30 1946 as the first date and September 14 as the last. Scarlet fever is about the same on the later date as on the earlier, dysentery also about the same, diphtheria a trifle higher, gonorrhœa considerably higher, syphilis much higher, tuberculosis about a third higher, and typhoid nearly double. But what really matters most is a more generalised degeneration in the health and strength of the whole community.

My own view may be summed up in the words of a British M.O.H. who suddenly "let himself go" at a mess in Hamburg one Sunday afternoon. "What on earth are you politicians in London up to?", he said, mistaking my occupation. "Do you realise what's going on here? Ignoramuses see some people in the streets looking fairly well nourished but don't realise that they are living on carbohydrates and have no resistance, and they forget that the most seriously undernourished people are at home. The present figure of tuberculosis is appalling, and it may be double next year. An epidemic of any kind would sweep everything before it. We are on the edge of a frightful catastrophe: and if you politicians in London"—he looked at me indignantly, and swept my disclaimer aside—"don't do something about it very soon two problems that seem to have been worrying you will be solved. The size of the German population and manure."

1. The bunker school at Düsseldorf.

2. Inside the bunker school.

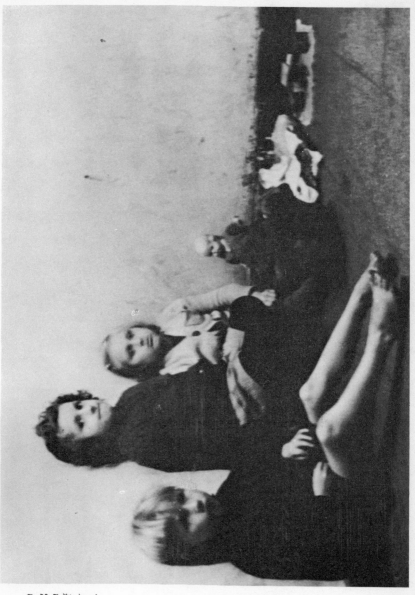

3. Children playing "home" in a corridor of the bunker school.

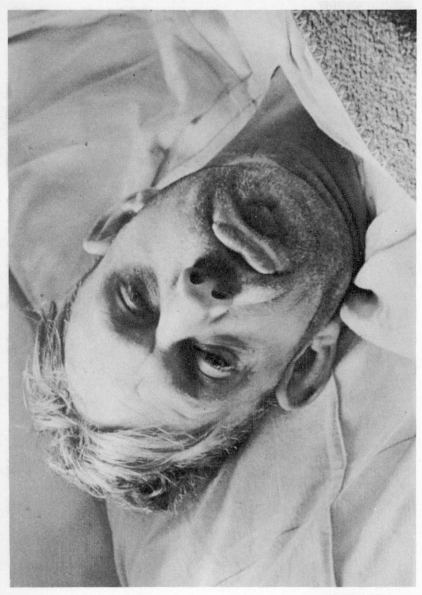

4. The face of the man with the swollen scrotum.

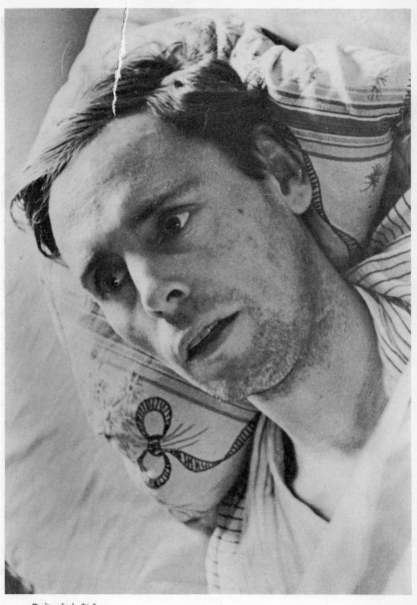

5. The man in the University Hospital, Hamburg— "penicillin not permitted."

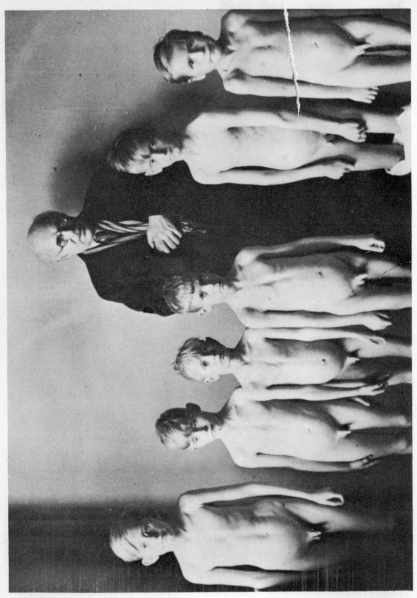

6. Children chosen for a "recovery home" at an elementary school in Hamburg.

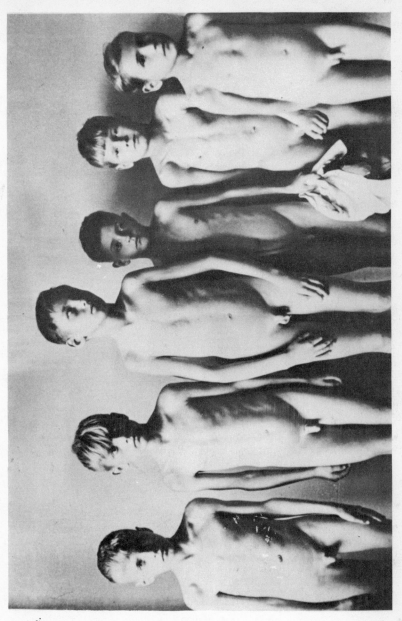

7. The same.

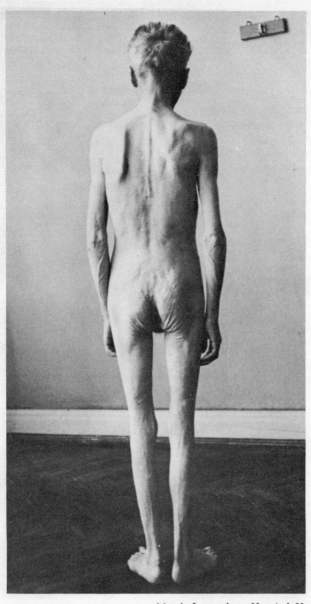

8. Man in Langenhorn Hospital, Hamburg.
Emaciation, not œdema. 56, looked 70. Was
clearing rubble, and got half heavy workers' ration.
Unmarried, as are many of these cases—
they depend on eating "out."

9. Woman recovering from œdema in Town
Hospital, Düsseldorf. Had been there three weeks.
Husband dead, lived with her brother entirely
on ration card. Water nearly gone.

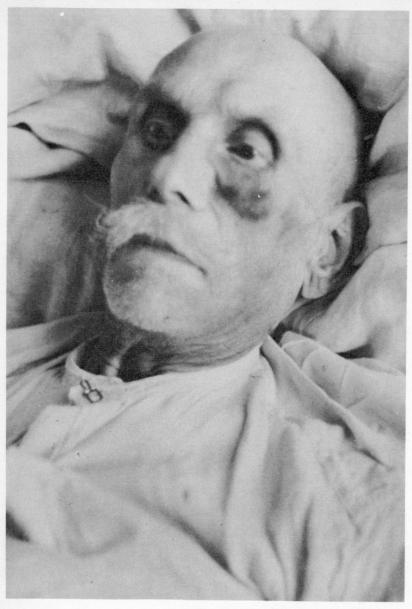

10. Emaciation (not œdema) case in Town
Hospital, Düsseldorf. Came three weeks before—
collapsed and fell: see mark on face.

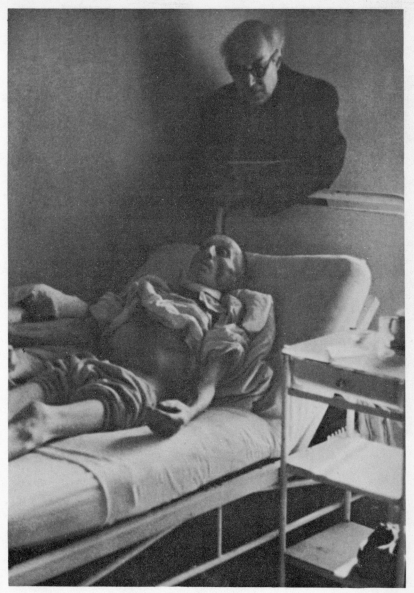

11. *In Town Hospital, Düsseldorf. Came in two months before; water now gone. Alone; baker.*

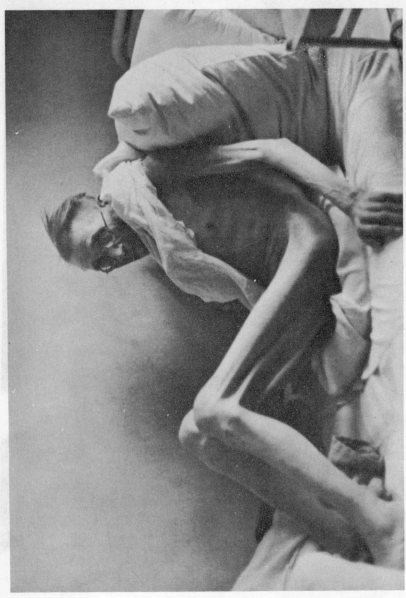

12. In Town Hospital, Düsseldorf. Had been there eight weeks. Water now gone. Homeless bachelor.

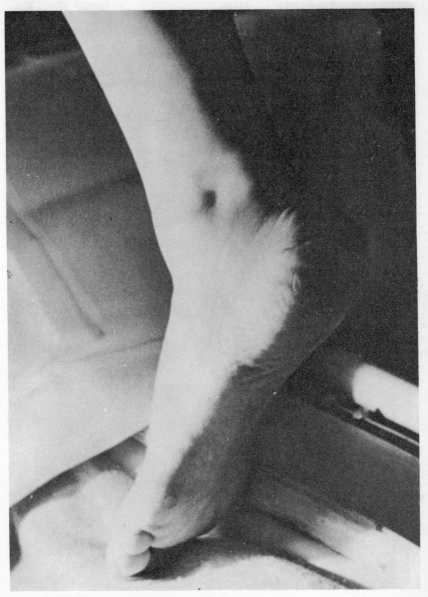

13. Foot of a man who had come to University
Hospital, Hamburg, four weeks before with œdema.
Now all water gone except a little in foot. I made
the dent that you see.

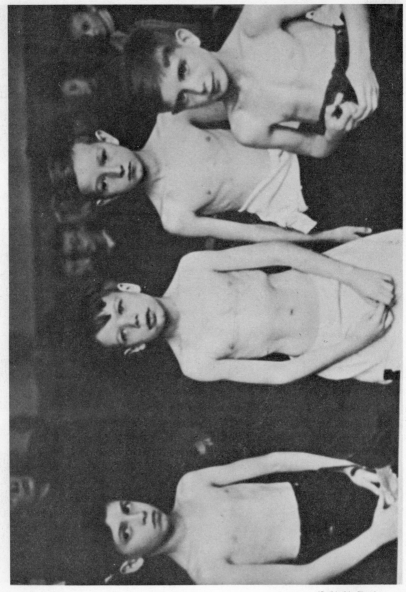

14. Boys undressed at my request at a school in Düsseldorf.

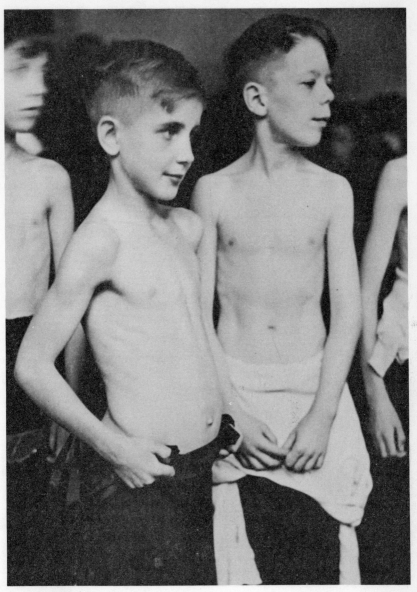

15. The same.

16. The children of the Oberhausen mother who "broke down."

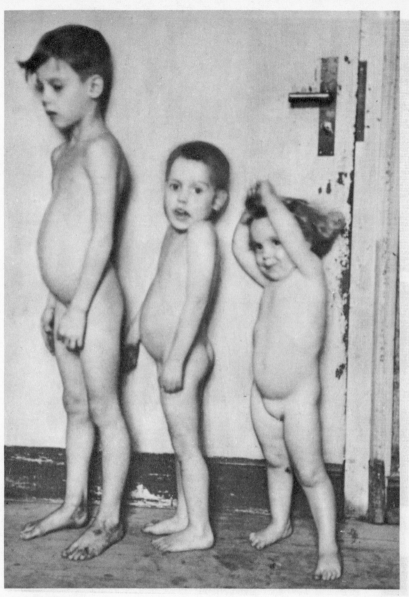

17. The same.

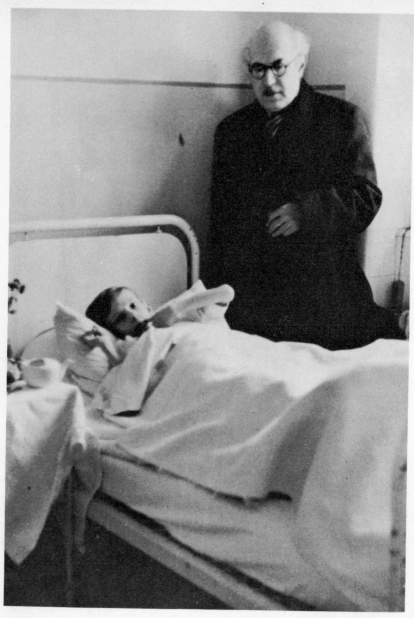

18. Child of ten dying from TB
in the Town Hospital, Düsseldorf.

II

SHOES AND OTHER THINGS

§ (i)

"THIS MISERY OF BOOTS"

(From The Daily Herald, Nov. 30)

W<small>HEN</small> I <small>WAS</small> in my early teens, a very famous Fabian pamphlet was published called *This Misery of Boots*. H. G. Wells was the author. For thirty years or more I had forgotten all about it: but the title rang in my head day after day and hour after hour in Hamburg and Düsseldorf and Oberhausen and a dozen other places. It is ringing in my head still.

Attention has been almost exclusively concentrated on the desperate food situation in Germany, but food is by no means the whole story. The working class has been wearing out its last articles of necessity, and the possibilities of replacement have, for a large majority, just not existed. The result is literally indescribable: you can only understand what it means when you actually see it—or, at a long remove, by photographs.

I can deal here with only two of the most urgent necessities. The first is children's shoes. I went into school after school in Germany, taking classes at random and simply asking children with *kaputten*—ruined—shoes to put up their hands. Here are a few of the results: 34 out of 58, 15 out of 37, 34 out of 53. (Incidentally, 50 per cent. of the latter had had no breakfast—and, during the bread famine in the Rhineland, this was a common occurrence.) I then got the children to come up to the front, and had a look at their feet. Now glance, please, at the photographs (plates 19–42) for specimens of what I saw. There's no fake about them—it's my hand that you see holding the children's legs.

Bits of dirty rag: a thin strap over a stocking full of holes: soles—innumerable soles—completely broken away from the uppers—these were common form. Then there were the children hobbling painfully in shoes borrowed from a younger brother: and children slopping about in their mother's or father's shoes: and, in one class, three children completely barefooted. One child said he wouldn't be able to come to school tomorrow "because father would want his shoes": another—"I have Hans' shoes so he's got to stay at home". The teachers estimated that, when the really wet weather started, "shoe absentee-ism" might amount to 50 per cent.

That is what I saw with my own eyes: but still I wasn't satisfied. I saw it, truly, in class after class and town after town: but, I said to myself desperately, mightn't this after all be a bad sample—could it conceivably be typical of the zone as a whole? So I thought I'd try statistics for a change. Now the official figure of the number of children's shoes needed for the period from July to December, at the very minimum and on the most "Spartan" plan possible—not on the basis of civilised living—is 6,200,000: and the total number of *Bezugsmarken* issued for their purchase, from May to December (actual figure to November, estimated for December), is 1,771,000. So, at our Commerce Headquarters at Minden, cold figures on a half-sheet of notepaper confirmed, and for the whole zone, the human tragedy that I had been witnessing during the last few weeks.

I will take only one other article of necessity. I think I might have asked about it anyhow, for when you see these children at "school" in an air-raid bunker without fresh air or daylight, you suddenly think of what your own children looked like 17 or 26 years ago. But there was no necessity to ask: whomever you might be talking to, whether it was a doctor, or a British or German welfare worker, or one of our own people concerned with the distribution of consumer goods, sooner or later, and nearly always sooner, the same topic would come up—the topic of babies' napkins. *Babies' napkins, to all intents and purposes, simply do not exist.* 520 babies were born in Düsseldorf in October, but not a single *Bezugsmark* was issued for the purchase of a napkin. In Essen, during the same month, 700 babies were born; 25 *Bezugsmarken* were issued—and it was the first issue for five months.

There is a similar appalling shortage of everything else that babies need. As to the clothing position generally, here are figures about textiles as a whole. Permitted Potsdam level of production, a trifle under 19,000 tons a month: present capacity, 15,700 tons a month: actual production, 4,000 tons a month. By the end of the year stocks of raw material will be practically exhausted, and then, unless something's done about it, the whole thing will come to an end. The remedy—import raw material and stop exporting coal.

And now, I suppose, someone who imagines he's an Englishman in the real sense as well as by the accident of birth will say "They've brought it on themselves". The babies too?

§ (ii)

MORE FACTS ABOUT CONSUMER GOODS

In a conversation with a high British authority in Schleswig-Holstein (October 7th) I was shown a list of items of clothing, etc., needed as a matter of desperate urgency for the "expellees" there, who number about 1,200,000 out of a total population of 3,000,000. Examples: men's overcoats 200,000; shoes 1,000,000; men's drawers

400,000; women's overcoats 200,000; women's knickers 400,000; sanitary towels 150,000; blankets 500,000. My informant added that he hoped, at best, to get 10 per cent. of these requirements. The minimum need for beds for these "expellees" was about 360,000, of which about 15,000 were being obtained. I visited a ship and a large camp in which "expellees" were housed, and saw mostly stretchers, wooden bunks, and bundles of sordid bed-clothes on the floor: indeed, now that I come to think of it, I don't recollect seeing a single bed. But my memory may be at fault.

In Hamburg (October 10th) a senior officer told me that the "Spartan" needs of the general population in that city were being met to the extent of no more than 10 per cent. I should add that there was an improvement over the zone as a whole in November, when there was an exceptional issue of *Bezugsmarken* to dispose of accumulated stocks. But this improvement, though considerable in absolute figures, was quite insignificant relatively to the need.

The senior inspector of high-schools for girls in Hamburg told me (October 11th) that it was impossible to get children's clothes mended, as there were no mending materials—no wool, cotton, needles, etc. Even in middle-class homes such things as toothbrushes, combs and sponges were lacking. Sanitary towels were quite unobtainable.

I was told in Hamburg (October 15th) by the German public health officer, in the presence of the British public health officer, who did not demur, that in this city (*a*) the supply of bandages satisfied only one fifth or one sixth of the demand, there being hardly enough to cover even fresh wounds; (*b*) there was sufficient insulin to meet only one third of the requirements; (*c*) in addition to insulin and penicillin, plaster of Paris, iodine, bismuth, alcohol and digitalis were all in short supply. 80,000 men, at the date given, were without artificial legs, and some had been waiting for three or four years.

During a tour of homes, bunkers, night-refuges etc. in Hamburg I found innumerable cases of people sleeping four in one bed ("foot to foot"); on the floor; on wood, covered with a thin and dirty bit of sacking filled with straw or sawdust; and on stretchers. I shall give examples later. I found incredibly filthy bedclothes, and sometimes only a single blanket for covering, or no covering at all.

At a conference with students of Hamburg University (October 19th) I learned that a recent census had shown that only 50 per cent. of them had a stove.

Contraceptives are virtually unobtainable.

I was told at a conference in Düsseldorf with the German public health officer for North Rhine–Westphalia and four other doctors, including the director of children's hospitals, that expectant mothers came to lie in with nothing at all for their babies, and that the nurses went scrounging round for bits of cloth in which the mothers could wrap up their babies when they left.

Gelsenkirchen is a town of 260,000 inhabitants. Here is a list of *Bezugsmarken* issued for June—the total list, I think, of all *Bezugsmarken*, but possibly the totals only for the articles named: 56 cardigans, 49 frocks, 21 knickers, 4 babies' napkins, 3 babies' knickers, 3 rubber sheets, 7 kilograms of knitting wool, and 21 small bath towels. There were 182 births during the same period.

The chief doctor of a Red Cross hospital near Cologne urgently requested (September 21st) the following articles for sick "expellees" who could not be admitted without them: 25 mattresses, 80 sheets, 80 pillow-cases, 100 towels, 60 children's night-clothes, and so on. The answer was that "nothing could be done".

When I was with the British welfare officer for Düsseldorf (October 30th) a haggard and yellow-faced woman came in, and you could hardly hear what she said for her sobbing. Her two children had no shoes: she had been applying to the *Wirtschaftsamt* for *Bezugsmarken* since February, and had just been told to apply again next year. One of her children had died of undernourishment in 1943. As she was a cleaner at the Control Commission office, and special things can be done for such people, the welfare officer wrote her an order.

I select a few items (out of over 100 headings) in the "Spartan bid" put in for the third quarter of 1946 by the British welfare branch at Düsseldorf. The articles were wanted for "expellees" in Westphalia, and you must remember that they arrive, these victims of wickedness, all but naked, for the most part, of possessions. 30,000 women's overcoats, 35,000 women's knickers, 45,000 pairs of women's stockings, 5,000 pairs of women's shoes, 100,000 sanitary towels, 10,000 pairs of boys' trousers, 18,000 boys' vests, 30,000 girls' dresses, 30,000 infants' sets (0–18 months), 70,000 blankets, 40,000 towels, 60,000 sheets, 80,000 chairs, 180,000 knives, forks and spoons, 100,000 plates, 60,000 cooking-pots, and so on. The total number of articles in the list was 3,118,000. By October 30th not a single article had been received.

I have before me an official document issued at Düsseldorf for the Regional Economic Officer, Military Government, North Rhine–Westphalia, and dated October 28th 1946. It includes a table giving (*a*) the estimated yearly requirements for the region ("based on a minimum scale which is below that at which normal peace requirements are assessed"), and (*b*) the *Bezugsmarken* issued from May to November inclusive. It must be remembered that the latter figures include the exceptional November issue. In the figures that follow the first is the (*a*) and the second the (*b*) figure. Men's and boys' clothing: 33,283,000; 1,982,000. Women's and girls' clothing: 38,623,000; 1,425,000. Boys' clothing (4 to 15 years): 6,727,000; 584,000. Babies' clothing: 1,716,000; 355,000. House and table linen: 22,166,000; 1,166,000. Babies' bedding: 231,000; 61,000. Furniture: 3,143,000; 190,000.

I'm told that people don't "understand" statistics. They're really quite simple. Those just given mean, for instance, that only one out of every 16 girls and women who desperately need some garment—"Spartan" implies "desperately"—can get it.

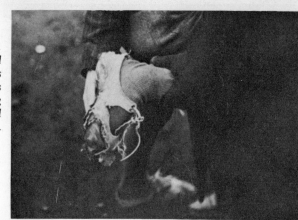

19 (and to **42**).
*School
children's
shoes
in Hamburg
and
Düsseldorf.*

20

21

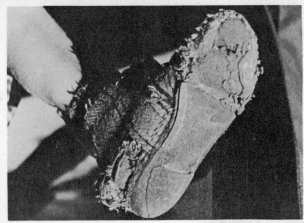

22

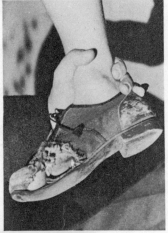

23

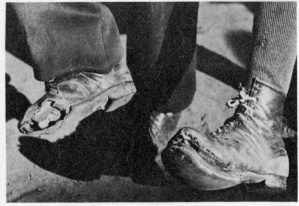

24

25

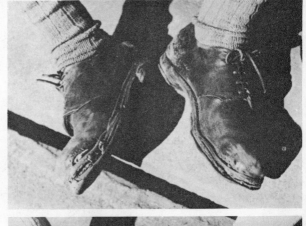

26

27

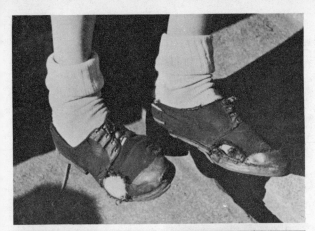

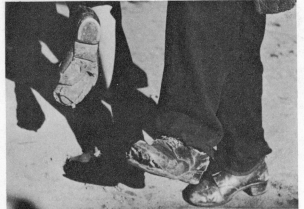

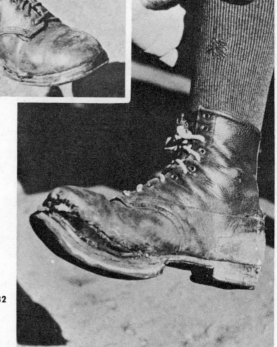

33

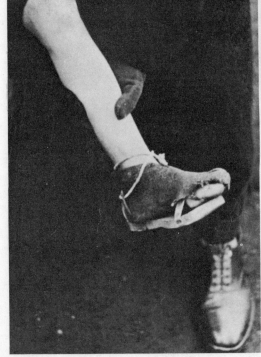

34

35

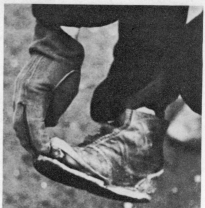

36

37

38

39

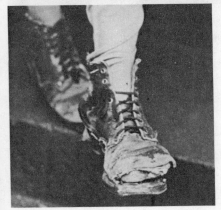

40

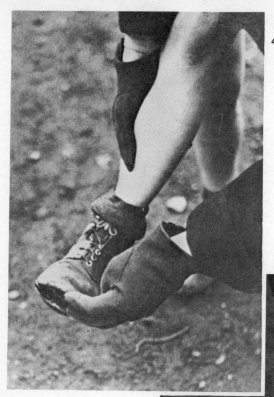

41

42

III

PEOPLE'S HOMES

LETTER WRITTEN TO MY WIFE

Friday October 25th,
Hamburg, 5.45 a.m.

I WANT TO try to get on to paper what I saw last night.
I went with the Salvation Army people, who are doing a
wonderful work, to investigate one or two cases that had
been brought to their attention, and then to see the
cellar-dwellings generally.

In one room—I'll describe the size presently—were
living a soldier discharged at the beginning of October,
his wife (who is expecting a baby in a fortnight) and his
seventy-two year old mother. They live, eat, cook, work,
and sleep in the one room. There is one bed: a table: two
chairs: a very small side-table: and a little cooking-stove.
The amount of space, apart from that taken up by this
furniture, is about *32 square feet*—about 2×2 between the
table and the door, 5×2 between table and bed, and 6×3
between table, wall and stove.

The old mother sleeps in the bed; *on the floor*, on a filthy
rug but no mattress, sleep the husband and wife—who will
have a baby in a fortnight. They sleep in the 6×3 space.
I asked the wife whether she could sleep: she smiled quite
bravely, and shrugged her shoulders. Her clothes were
wretched, and she was barefoot; I asked her why, and
she showed me her only pair of shoes—a *kaputt* pair which
was more or less useless. She has no baby-clothes or

cradle—nothing. People like this have literally *nothing*. She will go to hospital for eight days and then return with her baby to this "room". Their chief concern is to get a basket or something to put the baby in—I suppose in the space I have marked 5×2, or on the table—people often sleep on tables in this Free City of Hamburg. They were all quite cheerful: I asked the old mother whether she had enough to eat, and she replied with a smile "Nein, nein, ich bin immer hungrig"—as if that were the fault of her appetite.

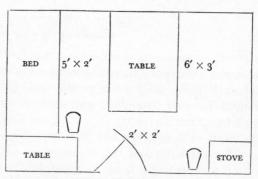

This was all pretty shaking: but it was heaven—I really mean this—in comparison with the next place, I think because the people were cheerful. The next place I can't begin to describe so as to convey any sense of it—it was like a deliberately vile Daumier cartoon. I doubt whether there could be more hopeless misery, or a more sordid caricature of humanity (humanity—the heights and depths: I told you in yesterday's letter of the Heiligenstadt Testament which I saw the night before last—they had kept it back for me, guarded by two men night and day, to do me honour). Then I try to restore my sense of proportion by remembering that Belsen and Auschwitz were far, almost infinitely, wickeder.

The place was a cellar under rubble in one of the huge

devastated areas. For light (during the day) and air there was one tiny window. On a table was a sort of open lamp with a naked flame—some sort of kerosene affair. There was one bed about the size of mine at home, in which the wife and husband were sleeping; on a sort of couch was the son, crippled in the war, and I should say in the twenties; and on the floor, on an indescribably filthy "mattress" which was all broken open with the sawdust spilling out, was the daughter. She looked fifty, but I suspect she was about twenty-five. This was an extraordinary creature. Imagine E— A—, but taller and gaunter, with a huge nose (or it looked huge), a bony emaciated face, and several front teeth missing, and you get an idea of what she looked like in the half-light of the lamp. I imagine that she ought to have been rather handsome— perhaps a little like Livia. She also appeared to be pretty crippled, and her hand was shaking terribly, I suppose from hunger. There was no free space in the cellar at all— and again they lived, ate, and slept here. Nobody could work—the young man couldn't because he was crippled, and the father because he was too weak. They lived on the father's tobacco card: it brought them in 120 marks every six weeks to supplement their wretched dole—40 cigarettes at three marks apiece. (German cigarettes are much less valuable than English, which are fetching seven marks.) The black market here *keeps people alive*. The air was so thick that I could hardly keep my glasses free enough from steam to see. The woman cried when the Salvation Army people gave her some money—and we all hurriedly unloaded our cigarettes, with a sort of personal shame, on the young man. And now I haven't given the least idea of the nightmare sordid horror of the whole thing: there was no cheerfulness here, and I am quite sure I shall never forget the huge trembling half-toothless daughter—who might have looked like Livia.

When we left this hell of a place, we picked our way over piles of rubble by the light of a torch; on all three sides you could see an occasional feeble speck of light on the ground, which showed that some of the cellar-dwellers were awake.

We then went a little further on, where there were cellars under ruined buildings by the canal—horribly damp. In one cellar—this one was marvellously clean—were sleeping seven people—a mother, father, twins of twenty, twins of eight, and one other child. (Plate 130.) The mother, who sat up in bed to talk to us, was wonderfully brave, God bless her. The son of twenty had just come in—he was some sort of metal worker—they showed us one of the irons (for ironing clothes) he makes. His dinner was on the table—a medium-sized plate of mixed cabbage and mashed potatoes. I asked him when he had had his last meal—it was now half-past ten. He had had it at twelve—the same dish of cabbage and potatoes; for breakfast six slices of bread with smear. I foolishly asked whether he had had any butter; he laughed in amazement—but not at all bitterly. The Salvation Army people gave the woman a large bar of chocolate, and just as we were leaving we heard one of the children asking for it. It is quite impossible to give you any idea of what it means to these people to be given a little extra food like that.

My dear, all this is not exceptional. In Hamburg, I am told (I haven't checked this yet), there are 77,000 people living in bunkers, cellars, etc.; and the Salvation Army adjutant, who has been working here for a year and a half, estimates that 25% of them are living under "Daumier" conditions. The official statistics show that the general housing position in Hamburg is frightful.

The Salvation Army people stopped as we were driving back to show me one of the tiny "graves" with which the place is dotted—a little cross with "here rests our mother . . ." and a withered wreath by the side of the "road" (Plate 57). The mother had been buried under the debris, and of course the body is still there—there must be hundreds of thousands of bodies under the rubble. The three nights of our mass raids must have been worse than hell (and I remind myself again that Belsen and Auschwitz were far worse). Blazing people threw themselves into the Canal. There is a mass grave near here where, the Salvation Army people told me, 20,000 people are buried.

Oh my dear, get copies of this made and send them to John Strachey and Attlee. They are both decent and kind-hearted men; and if only they could see what I have seen they would let us send parcels of food to these poor and dear people—I call them dear, because their suffering, and often their bravery, make one love them: or is it that loving them is the only way to save one's own self-respect as a human being? How *can* they let bread-rationing in England be an excuse, when we know that so many changed their B.U.s into points? And these parcels are *not* a little thing: each individual case is each individual case: and I have seen with my own eyes the gratitude with which even a single bar of chocolate is received. It is a terrible sin to withhold the power to give this solace. If John could fly here and see for a single night what I have seen, he would make whoever it is in the Cabinet that is obstructing give way.

You know I went to Belsen on Tuesday, and I wrote to you what I felt; I don't for a single second forget the other side of the picture. But these are people in an agony of suffering—and some of our authorities at home are behaving less well than the "other ranks" of the B.A.O.R. who take buns from the canteen and give them to the children.

43. The home of the girl with a headache at Jülich.

44. The same.
Entrance.

45. The same.
The window.

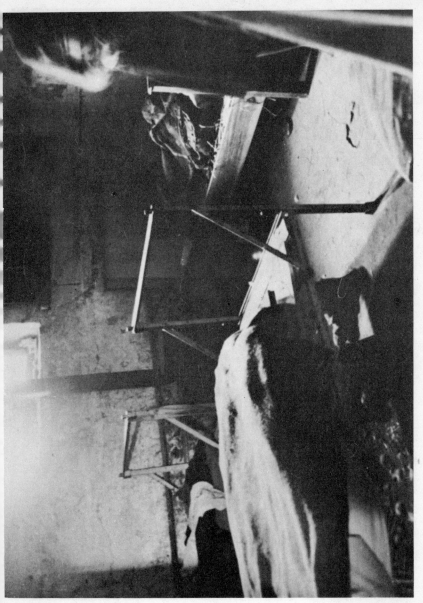

46. The same.
The bedroom.

47. Jülich.
The home of
the woman
who wanted
to die.

48. The same.
Lavatory.

49. The same.

50. The same.
The shoe.

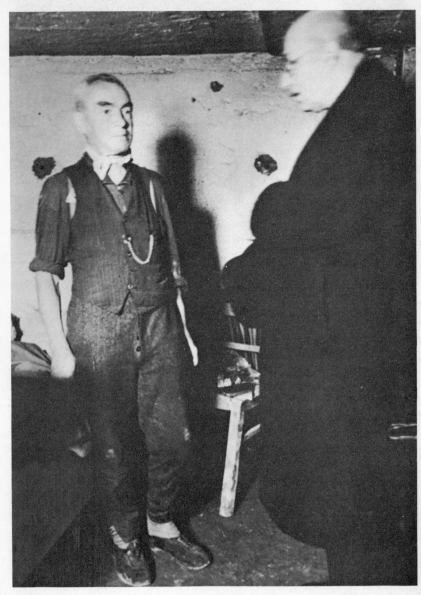

51. Jülich. The man with the carbuncles.

52. Jülich. These six did everything in this room: wooden walls, leaking roof of wood and paper. 162 square feet. Old man 84. TB feared for one child.

53. The same
—outside. The
room on the
right cannot
be used, even
by Jülich
standards.
Stadtdirektor
by my side.

54. Hotel-
Restaurant
Kaiserhof,
Jülich.

55. *High Street, Düren.*

56. *Düren.*

57. This is a grave at Düren, similar to the Hamburg
ones described in the text.

LITTLE JÜLICH

On your way from Düsseldorf to Aachen you come upon what is perhaps the most ruined town in Germany. Jülich is 93 per cent. destroyed; our bombers came over one night, and after twenty minutes it was no longer there. I think of it as "little Jülich", and with a curious mixture of sadness and affection.

I was the first Englishman to visit it for four months, and my arrival on a Sunday morning caused quite a flutter of excitement. I found my way with difficulty to the modest town hall, for many of the streets, of course, no longer exist. A small delegation, which included the Stadtdirektor, received me charmingly, and wanted to give me particulars of "Jülich then and now"; but I had an early appointment at Aachen, and was impatient to be gone. I stayed, when it came to it, for two or three hours.

We began to walk among the rubble, and I asked how many people had lived there before the war. "Eleven thousand," said the Stadtdirektor, who talked very fair English with an attractive hesitation. "And now?" I thought the answer would be a few hundred, but I was out by seven thousand or so. I wondered, but didn't ask, where they might be living.

A minute later we came upon a sort of stove-pipe sticking out of the ground. The Stadtdirektor knew the place, but it took us a little time to find the entrance to what was clearly some kind of underground dwelling. After one or two false starts we went, with my torch shining, down a narrow incline tunnelled in the earth; and suddenly, by some trick of childhood recollection, I thought of the "gaps" at Margate.

The cellar consisted of two tiny rooms housing seven people. Six of them were in what I suppose must be called the sitting-room, which was about the height of a man;

they could just cram into it—the parents, two adult sons, and two younger children (the seventh was out). One of the children was sitting with her aching head bent down over the table, and she didn't look up even when I had a photograph taken. I have wanted many things in my life, some good and some bad: but what I wanted just for that second more passionately than I ever wanted anything before—I've no doubt I'm exaggerating, but that's how it seemed—was a bottle of aspirin. Back now in London, and going to the Ivy for lunch and so on, I suddenly catch myself thinking at odd moments that while I am here they are there—all of them still there in that cellar, and the girl perhaps with a headache that will never go away.

In the adjoining hole you could just make out a dim hell of wooden beds and dirty bedclothes. They had neither water nor lavatory: for excreting they used either a pail or, more commonly, the rubble outside. The clothes they "stood up in" seemed their only possessions. (Plates 43–46.)

Up and across what had once been a road a bit of a small house was standing—a ground-floor room and two rooms above it, with the staircase (now an outside stair-case) intact, but the rest of the house a mess of bricks open to the sky. A mother and daughter lived and slept in the tiny ground-floor room, and I can't get them out of my mind either. The girl was a bad case of open TB, with brooding eyes and a half-open mouth: the mother looked so desolate and grey with sorrow that I oughtn't to have been horrified, as I was, when she told us she wanted to die. She was a widow, and the two of them lived on some-thing microscopic. The woman was barefoot, for she possessed only a single ruined shoe. I asked her to come into the doorway to be photographed with the shoe in her hand, but she wouldn't come far forward into the good light, saying that she didn't want to make a show of herself. God knows that whenever I took a photograph I made the interpreter explain that I was doing it only to help, for people who wouldn't believe my descriptions might believe photographs; but even so I always felt horribly ashamed. (Plates 47–50.)

Underground nearby lived a man of 69, alone. His wife was dead, and he had heard nothing of his sons for two years: they might be prisoners, he thought, in Russia. There was no artificial light in his cell, and for natural light only a hole a foot or so across and covered with paper. The ceiling was wet. As I flashed my torch about I noticed the filthy bandage on the man's neck, and saw that his hands were swollen and covered with those corrupt-looking spots—something midway between impetigo and small carbuncles—which I had already seen so frequently during the last few days, especially among the children. They appear to have cleared up, it seems, and then new ones break out on the half-healed scars. (Plate 51.)

All this was the dreadful side of Jülich: and it wasn't exceptional, as you'll appreciate when you remember that seven thousand people are living there, and hardly a house even partially standing. But there was a happy side too. I had been getting friendly with my Stadtdirektor, who turned out to be a Social Democrat, and to have been "on the run" continuously from 1933 right up to what he still called, in spite of everything, the liberation. He was a gentle little man, and when he found me sympathetic asked if he might come in my car as far as Düren (on the way to Aachen) so as to be able to talk a little longer. As we were leaving the rubble for the green fields, I noticed a longish bungalow of wood that seemed somehow to gleam and glisten in that awful desolation: and over the door the words, in bold lettering, "Hotel-Restaurant Kaiserhof". I looked at my comrade with a gesture of enquiry, and he replied with a smile, half proud and half deprecating, *Es beginnt* ("Something's beginning"). I got out to have a look. Two or three men were drinking a glass of beer in the vestibule-restaurant, and we sat and talked with them for a moment or so. Then we went down the corridor. The rooms that opened out of it on both sides were small, overcrowded, and furnished with the minimum of necessities; but they were bright and clean, and the people seemed contented. In one room there was a mother with the three most beautiful children I have ever seen. (Plate 54.)

On the road to Düren my comrade, who had been feeling his way, began to talk more freely. "Couldn't the British comrades" he said "come to see us occasionally? There are a lot of socialists here, and we feel terribly cut off. I don't mean official visits from Morgan Phillips [I was surprised that he knew the name]; I mean the little socialists." A few minutes later, for by this time I had told him I was a publisher, he begged me to send him some English books. "And up-to-date newspapers," he added. "At present I only get an Observer four months old. I want to tell my people about what's happening in England, but it's difficult to do it when my news is so out of date." He always called the inhabitants of Jülich "my people" as if he were a sort of priest; and indeed in one sense he was.

Shortly afterwards we arrived at Düren and he left me. I don't suppose I shall ever see Jülich again. But I want to; and I wonder whether I have at all made clear why I think of it as "little Jülich", and with a curious mixture of sadness and affection.

§ (iii)

MORE ABOUT PEOPLE'S HOMES

I have reproduced above a letter to my wife exactly as it was written, in an attempt to convey the impression made on me at the time. A few more descriptions may be useful.

On October 11th, in Hamburg, I visited a number of those "emergency" buildings of one kind or another which, eighteen months after victory, still house tens of thousands of human beings. The first was a great building of concrete, hellishly grim, and divided into a number of big, high and almost utterly bare rooms. Six people lived in the first of the rooms we went into—parents, a girl of 22, and sons of 7, 10 and 14. There was, of course, no sort of privacy—they hadn't even been able to fix up screens or curtains. You're shocked by that sort of thing at first, and then, when you come up against it time after time, you no longer notice it. The plank beds had, for mattresses, dirty sacks which were either empty or filled with wood shavings. There had been, until recently, only one blanket for each person, but now there were two or three. These people had been living here since January, and I was told by the housing authorities that there was no chance of their being able to move out for at least another year. The father was in—he had heart disease, and was unable to move about. For furniture there was a tiny stove, a table and six stools —nothing, not even a single upright chair, to rest their backs against. The walls were loathsome. (Plates 58, 59.)

But there are degrees of misery; and a little crockery and so forth on a wooden shelf somehow connected the place with human beings. There was nothing of the kind in the next room. Seven people lived in this—the parents and five children, aged between 4 and 12. They had lost their rooms in 1943, gone to Brandenburg, returned in December '45, and had been here since February. There were no shavings in the sacks that covered their sleeping-planks, and the rest of the furniture consisted of three stools and one small table. Only two of them were at home—the mother and a child of 9, neither of whom had shoes or stockings. Remember, please, that the floor was of rough concrete. The mother was an older version of the half-paralysed girl I described in the letter to my wife: she was crippled by rheumatism, and had what I put down in my notes as a "swivel eye", which oozed horribly. They were eating better than some I came across: they had had potatoes and tea for breakfast and three slices of bread each with a little butter at eleven, and the remaining meal was to consist of swedes and potatoes. I find most of my photographs inadequate, because the photographer was such a brilliant artist that he just couldn't help getting an effect of beauty even out of what was disgusting and vile; but plate 60 does give some idea of this particular corner of hell.

We went on to a bunker. Bunkers are air-raid shelters divided into rooms or cells; a few are underground, but most of them tower up before you, great concrete masses spotted with diminutive vents that look like the eyes of the blind. The Gertigstrasse bunker was of this type. The heat and stench—or not so much stench as a kind of solid and continuous wall of congealed bad breath—were appalling. The rooms contained nothing but tiers and tiers of wooden bunks, with sometimes a bench and table; here the inmates not only slept but lived, when they were in. There was a small kitchen for the whole bunker. One room housed 8 men—until very recently it had housed 16; and in another of the same size, for women, 15 had been living a fortnight before. In a tiny cell, hardly bigger than its occupant, a man lived quite alone. (Plates 61–63.)

A longish drive took us to the Stadtpark, which used, I was told, to be a series of beautiful lawns. Now Nissen huts seem to crowd every inch of it. Eating in one of them was a miscellany of men shanghaied in other provinces—quite legally, of course—for work on the Hamburg Project; in another a medley of men, women, children and babies, prisoners of war from a camp in Norway under our control, were awaiting orders to move on. They were going to the Russian zone, and had been here six weeks. (Plate 64.)

The last place on our list that day was the Langenhorner Chaussee. The wooden huts there were occupied by homeless Hamburgers. In one room there were 18 of them, including 10 children and belonging to 6 different families. These people, all jumbled up together, were making the best of it; I noticed a bunch of flowers in a glass on the table, and four plants in pots on what looked like a radiogram in the corner.   (Plates 65 and 66.)

. . . . .

These were some of the "emergency" buildings—the "emergency" being a matter of months or years. Seven days later I went to have a look at ordinary housing conditions in Hamburg. In the first room we went to—one room for everything—there was a mother with 4 children, whose ages ran from 4 to 9. The husband was a prisoner in Russia, and the wife got a dole which came out at about 100 marks a month after the rent was paid. What she wanted above all was shoes for the children. She was a lovely creature—spiritually, I mean, for I can't remember what she looked like physically, except that she smiled the whole time. "I'm doing my best for the children" she said "so that when my husband comes home he'll have nothing to reproach me with." God, how I hated at that moment the cruelty and treason of men, who, with the war over, can so offend by holding their prisoners for a year, for two years, for three years, and perhaps forever.

In the Kleine Marienstrasse, opposite a waste of desolation, a man had got hold of some bricks and made a dwelling-place with them out of a ruin. He had a wife, 7 children and a dog. The first of the two rooms measured 105 square feet; the leaky ceiling was made of cardboard and corrugated paper over bits of timber. This was the living room. The mother and father slept here in a narrow bed, which for once in a way had a mattress of sorts, filthy and ruined though it was. The other room measured 85 square feet. Three children slept in each of the two beds, "foot to foot"; there was also a pram. Each bed had an eider-down and a sordid, wet, coverless pillow. The zinc roof was soaking. They had neither water nor lavatory, but used the rubble opposite.

The elections had just been held, and I asked the man how he had voted. "S.P.D. (Socialist)." "Why?" "Be-cause I wanted a change—no more Nazis." He had deserted during the war, but the Gestapo had "come after" his wife and he had returned to save her and been imprisoned for 6 months. He was a shoemaker by trade, and his spirit was marvellous. (Plates 67–75.)

Over in the Lammstrasse we found a flat with two rooms plus a diminutive communal kitchen. In the first room, which measured 110 square feet, a family of four did everything except cook. There was a bed for the widow and daughter of 18, a sofa for the son of 20, who was a rail-way worker, and the floor (without mattress) for the other daughter of 31. Their most treasured possession was a bicycle, which they kept in the room. "We manage" the woman said in reply to some question; "I have three very good children." On the table and ledges were pots of flowers, for it was the elder daughter's *Geburtstag*. (Plate 76.)

The other room was loathsome. The photograph gives some idea of it. The only free space was a narrow lane measuring three feet by ten, with on one side a jumble of sacks, bundles, winter potatoes and if I remember rightly coal—or perhaps the coal was outside the kitchen—and on the other side three beds with filthy bedclothes. Living in this room—I must repeat living, not merely sleeping in it—were a father and mother and five children. The father and a 13-year-old boy slept in the first bed; the mother with a 7-year-old boy and a 9-year-old daughter—at the foot—in the second; and two boys of 11 and 13 in the third. What the seven of them did with themselves when they were not in bed I can't imagine, for there was hardly room to stand, and nowhere at all to sit, either here or in the kitchen which they shared with the other family of four. And yet the father, a railwayman on night-shift who got out of bed to talk to me, was cheerful enough. The need of which he seemed most conscious was for cigarettes, as his ration ran to only one a day, and he couldn't afford to buy on the black market. When I gave him a few he was courteously grateful, and showed none of that obsequiousness which you read so much about but which I hardly ever came across, except in people who depended directly on the British for their jobs. All the railwaymen, he told me, were keenly interested in politics and had voted socialist almost without exception; he personally knew only one communist. The reason, he thought, was that they were always seeing prisoners of war returning from Russia in terrible shape—men looking as if they were 40 but turning out to be 21. This railwayman was one of the very few working-class people I met in Germany who were still, in the positive sense, pro-British. (Plates 77–79.)

In a cellar nearby, stiflingly hot, there were, exceptionally, four beds for four people—mother, father, and two children. But there was no room for anything else. (Plates 80 and 81.)

The next place we visited was a flat with two rooms and a kitchen, housing in all nine persons. In the first room, stuffy and squalid, two unrelated bachelors dossed down. The windows were smashed and boarded up with wood, and there was no natural light. Crammed together next door, with two beds between them, were a father and mother, two married daughters, and a child. But worst of all was the kitchen. Here, where everyone cooked, lived a married couple. The floor was rotten, and the room so small that when my conducting officer, the photographer and I had got in we almost literally could hardly turn round. The man was a communist, and had come out of a concentration camp—Fuhlsbüttel was the name of it, if I got it down right—in 1935. He had been unfit for work ever since, for they had put him for 72 hours in a cellar with a temperature of 5 degrees below zero, and had broken the base of his spine when they beat him. The only decoration in the room was a sort of poster he had made, with two red stars, crossed red flags, the words "ROT-FRONT" and "Unsterbliche OPFER", and drawings of Thaelmann, Schulze and Andrée. "My comrades" he said, pointing to it. I have said many bitter things about communists and shall say many more, for indeed I think that their philosophy, if it has its way, will ruin Europe; but I was able, thank God, to forget all about that and to call him "Genosse". I was grateful when he accepted my hand.

The other family called me away to show me the communal lavatory. I tried to excuse myself, but they insisted. It was at the bottom of a pitch-black staircase, or rather of half a one; for the stairs suddenly ended, and you had to jump on to a heap of bricks, and then walk a hundred yards or so on to the closet. When you had done, you had to jump back on to the stairs. The communist with the damaged spine, they told me, took an hour and a quarter every time he went. My photographer managed to get some sort of impression by the aid of my torch. (Plates 82–86.)

In the Repsoldstrasse we saw a bed- and living-room, almost the whole of it occupied by four beds, in which slept three girls of 10, 14 and 21, and two mothers, each with a baby. (Plates 87 and 88.) It was in this neighbourhood, I think, that a crowd gathered when people saw what I was up to, and a half-crazy woman seized my arm and dragged me off to show me something which my interpreter translated as "the mushrooms". They turned out to be some sort of fungus growing on the wet wall of her bedroom. "Ein Schweinerei" the woman kept screaming.

But the afternoon ended pleasantly. At Eppendorf, a suburb of Hamburg, a cheerful old labourer had built himself a little house—illegally, I gather—and added a small market garden. There were a few rabbits in a hutch, and some babies that seemed happy.

.　　.　　.　　.　　.

The same evening, after dining with the Burgomaster and Senate at the Rathaus—the modest dinner was excellently cooked, and they gave me one of the rare bottles of magnificent hock which the concierge had managed to hide from the Nazis—I went round the night refuges. These were places where you might spend only a single night. In the first of them were men who were wandering about from various parts of Germany; several of those I spoke to had been press-ganged for the Hamburg Project, and had got away from their barracks because they were dissatisfied with the conditions. I had seen one of them in the Stadtpark a few days before.

The second place was the Jahnturnhalle, where mothers and children were spending the night. They were units in that homeless crowd that goes milling about Germany "to find relatives", they said, but really, or mainly, I was told, because a restlessness has come over them that just won't let them settle down. (Plate 89.) In another room I talked to a boy from Pomerania with crippled feet. 3,000 young people, he said, had been sent to Cracow, and only 126 had returned. The rest were supposed to have ended up in Siberia, and so the young people were fleeing to the British zone. He had fled himself with 26 others, but only three had managed to get through. This story may, of course, have been "propaganda", but my conducting officer told me that week after week for months he had been hearing exactly the same. The Red Cross people, here or at one of the other refuges, told me that the place was much used by prisoners of war returning from the East. Many of them suffered from hunger œdema. They were given one piece of black bread as an emergency ration.

We finished at about two o'clock in the morning at a place called "The Asylum". (Plate 90.) A boy was leaving his bunk for the lavatory, and I got him to tell me his story. He was Georg Böhlmann, aged 16, of Wildstein near Eger, and a Sudeten German. He had been dancing with his friends one Sunday afternoon in the village when a car arrived full of Czech soldiers wearing armbands lettered, if I got it down right, S.N.B. They took away 43 boys—all Sudeten Germans—aged from 16 to 19. No reason was given.

The boys were taken to a mining camp near Brüx, where Böhlmann worked for 9 months, 8 or 9 hours a day and 7 days a week. They had a cup of coffee and one slice of bread for breakfast, 4 potatoes and sauerkraut at mid-day, and 2 slices of bread and a cup of coffee at 6. They were paid 20 Kronen a week, the price of a cigarette being 5 Kronen. They were not allowed to write home, and their parents had no knowledge of their whereabouts.

One day when the new ration of sauerkraut was being brought into the camp, Böhlmann seized the opportunity to escape with three others. (Of the 150 boys in the camp some tried to escape every week, but if they were caught they were beaten.) On September 1st he crossed the frontier near Bayreuth and made his way to Frankfurt-on-Main, mostly on foot, but sometimes by train—the latter "black", which meant, I gather, travelling on the luggage rack. From there he got to Hanover by canal boat, went to the Youth Labour Office for a job as an electrician, but failed as he was only an apprentice. So he came to Hamburg by lorry (I kept saying inside myself, with guilty insistence, "No, you never refused anyone a lift—or did you?") and was spending a night at the Asylum before trying again. He added that in Eger older men were similarly seized in the streets and taken off to labour camps. (Plate 91.)

. . . .

I left Hamburg for Düsseldorf on October 26th, and spent some of the following day—a Sunday—with the Red Cross detachment. I don t know how to describe these people and what they are doing; I can only say that I remember them with gratitude and happiness. They took me round some cellars. We went down two long flights of stairs to an awful couple of rooms below. There was, of course, no natural light, and no ventilation of any kind. The place, which had recently been flooded for 4 weeks, was inhabited by two women and five children, belonging to two different families. Every inch of room was crammed with furniture and beds in double tiers. The lavatory was a pail. I ventured into a wet, disused room with a curtain over the entrance; the stench was so frightful that I had to suck lozenges all the way back. One of the women was pregnant. A child, whose face was covered with sores, played with my torch and called me "uncle"; he wouldn't let me go. We visited cellar after cellar of this type; some of them were wonderfully clean, and on occasion decorated with home-made silhouette pictures, photographs and the like. Crucifixes were frequent. The worst place, I think, was a cellar of two rooms divided by a long wet passage, without light of any kind. A mother lived in one room, her daughter with several children in the other. They were cheerful. Down below, somewhere else, was an injured woman who couldn't move from her bed except with the aid of two sticks; she smiled at first, but presently began to sob, and kept repeating "Alles verloren". Many of these people had been bombed out two, three, or four times. All of them were grateful, terribly grateful, when they were given something.

The Red Cross people also took me to a bunker, of which there are several in Düsseldorf. This one was said to be the best, for there was a little passage between the double row of cells on each floor, and people could sit in it. The typical cell measured $2\frac{3}{4}$ lengths of my walking-stick by $4\frac{1}{2}$, and many contained five persons; that works out at about two square metres a person, or about $\frac{2}{5}$th of the Army minimum. There was of course no natural light, little or no ventilation, and the usual stench. I noticed one tiny box of a cell in which a one-legged man was living alone; he had neither electric light nor cover for his bed. All the children looked white, and many seemed consumptive. An old man in the passage was carefully gathering some home-grown tobacco into a little tin, and a woman was making a children's lamp for the forthcoming feast of St. Martin. The Control Commission housing officer for the area had made a little playground in front of the bunker for the children.

I made a more extensive tour of Düsseldorf dwelling-places towards the end of the week. Down a long dark staircase and then along a black tunnel was a man of 79, alone in a hole which he had made habitable—according to the ruling standards—"all by himself". His wife was out on the search for bread. In another part of the same cellar was a mother with three children—6, 10 and 14. All four of them slept in the only bed, two side by side in the ordinary way, and the other two side by side at the foot of it. The mother came back while we were there: it was 10.30, she had been queuing for bread since early morning, and had returned empty-handed—"bread nowhere". One of the children was still in bed; none had yet had anything to eat, as the last bread had gone yesterday. The father was a prisoner of war in Russia. Two of the children had TB. There was a tiny stove, but no coal or gas, only a little wood which they "fetched". For excretion they used a pail, which they emptied every morning into a hole they dug in the courtyard above. They had twice been bombed out. On one wall was a small faded photograph of the mother and father at their wedding, and on another some prince or king with the legend "Lerne leiden ohne zu klagen"—"Learn to suffer without complaining". (Plates 92 and 93.)

I thought I would leave the cellars, and have a look at what you might call more tolerable overcrowding. There was a room with a good cupboard and a few decent bits of furniture, and it would have been quite pleasant if you could have moved about in it. Nine people lived, slept and did their cooking there—a man and wife with five children of their own, the child of the man's sister, and his mother-in-law. They were all in except one of the children. The husband had been shot through the leg, had a stiff knee, and was unfit for work. He got 126 marks a month by way of relief and the mother-in-law got 22 marks; but as they had to pay 26 marks a month for rent, their money worked out at between 3 and 4 marks a week a head. They had bartered almost everything on the black market and now couldn't even take up the food on their ration cards, as two large cabbages, one of the women explained to me, cost three marks. None of them had had anything to eat that morning, but they were going to have five lbs. of potatoes and two or three onions between them for lunch. There was, as usual, no bread. The father had started on a job of home cobbling, and had been promised some vege-tables in payment. They all dressed up before being photo-graphed, and the mother, who was of a ghastly pallor, was particularly careful about her hair. All the children looked pasty. (Plate 94.)

.   .   .   .   .

On November 2nd I went to the mining town of Ober-hausen. Housing conditions here varied a good deal; in some cases they were fair, in many others—I went into shacks and flats at random—quite frightful. They had al-ways been pretty bad, I gathered, but had got worse owing to lack of repairs—you saw great gaping cracks, paper peeling from the walls, and the woodwork gone from the windows. Malnutrition and the shortage of household goods did the rest.

There were many overcrowded shacks, with for instance 9 people sharing 3 beds in 2 small rooms. (Plates 95 and 96.) The worst shack I saw was inhabited by a miner, his wife, and five children aged from 3 to 14. They had twice been bombed out, and now lived in three incredibly small rooms. It was half-past ten and a very cold morning, but one of the children was up in her nightdress, for the mother had been out shopping since daybreak. The young boy was going to be a miner; his shoes were broken open, and his jacket couldn't be mended as yarn was unobtainable. The mother's shoes were bad too, and only one of the other children had shoes at all, so they couldn't go to school. I can't remember whether all or only some of them had impetigo or scabies or whatever it is. The man had a carbuncle on his neck and the remains of many on his legs; this, I gather, is an occupational disorder, but is much aggravated by existing conditions. Each child had had a couple of slices of dry bread for breakfast; the midday meal for the whole nine of them was to consist of a few turnips and about five lbs. of potatoes, and then supper of potatoes and another couple of slices of dry bread apiece. "I wonder what Hynd would say about *this*?" said a well-known man who was with me. (Plates 97–103.)

Wherever you went in Oberhausen you saw spots and sores. A child's legs were covered with scars, some of them breaking open again (Plate 104); a miner had cut his knee, and the place wouldn't heal. When talking to him we discovered a horrible paradox. He had been ill for a month, and after the first ten days had lost his right to miners' ration and was now living as a "normal consumer". This was the ordinary practice. You would have said that to dock a man's food when he's ill is idiotic as well as iniquitous, and not at all the way to increase the output of coal. He had eaten two pieces of dry bread for breakfast and three potatoes and a few small mangel-wurzels for lunch. It was here I discovered that the so many grammes of skim milk were as mythical as the so many grammes of bread and so many grammes of cereals, for the family was getting only a quarter of its ration.

On the outskirts of this town there is a camp, in the main for people expelled from Polish-occupied Germany. Most of the inmates had been there for four months, and in a bunker for a similar period previously. It was a bitter, stormy day, and two or three dozen children were wandering about aimlessly in the soaking corridor. Some had ruined shoes and some had no shoes or stockings at all. (Plate 105.)

The living and sleeping quarters were small, bare concrete cells—or they looked and felt like concrete to me, but from my photographs you would judge them to be of white-washed brick. In one of them a mother and daughter were at their midday meal. The daughter looked 25, but turned out to be 16. The mother was in bed, very ill with what the girl thought was asthma or heart trouble or both: she could only speak in a whisper, but I gathered that what she complained about most was lack of air. I notice a window in the photograph, but I did not notice it at the time, for the place seemed stiflingly hot: perhaps it would have been too cold if they had opened the window, or perhaps they couldn't open it. The mother's weight had formerly been 70 kilos, but was now only 46, and in spite of her condition she got no extra food. They had each had two slices of dry bread for breakfast, and you can see in the photograph just how big was the plate of oats-and-water soup which was their whole lunch. These were not "expellees", but people bombed out from Oberhausen, evacuated to Bavaria, and now compelled to return. The mother, I think, will soon be dead. (Plate 106.)

In Aachen, which I visited later with the Friends Relief Service, the 22 bunkers are said to be among the worst in Germany, and the underground one I went over was certainly horrible, with its uniform series of unventilated cells measuring each about 70 square feet. In one of these lived a mother of 45, a son of 20, a son of 11 and a daughter of 9. There were only two narrow beds—there wouldn't have been room for more—and two slept in each of them, foot to foot. The son worked in the mines, and "was becoming weaker and weaker because he could get no rest". In another cell, with the usual two beds, a small stove and 21 square feet of free space, lived a man of 66 and his daughter of 39. "In former days anything so indecent would have been impossible" he muttered to me. (Plate 107.) But I have pleasant memories of this bunker, too. In a third cell was an old couple expelled from Silesia. They had lost everything, and even their clothes were borrowed; but it was Sunday, and by some exercise of care, or some trick of arrangement, the lady looked as she sat there exactly as my grandmother used to look when I went to tea with her on a Sabbath afternoon. They were beautiful, both of them—cheerful and dignified. A fourth cell, with the two beds again, was inhabited by a mother, a son of 16 (in the mines), a son of 12 and a daughter of 9. The husband was missing, and a third son was a prisoner of war. The boy of 12 was reading with extreme absorption *La Dame aux Camélias*, which he had picked up on a scrapheap, coverless and torn in two. He told me he loved reading, and I said I would send him some books. He at once jumped to his feet and held out his hand with the most charming of smiles. I felt as if he had given me his blessing.

. . . . .

To get the whole thing into perspective, how many of the say 23 million Germans in our zone are living in the sort of conditions I have tried, and I am sure quite failed, to describe? Certainly several millions, including many teachers, artists, students and professional men of one kind or another. On the other hand, a tiny and comparatively quite insignificant minority are still in possession of extremely comfortable establishments, inhabited by perhaps twice as many people as before but still with an amount of space unconscionable in existing conditions. The situation of the rest varies from very bad overcrowding in reasonably decent rooms, to something just adequate, or a trifle more or less than adequate, for modest human needs. This last category is a very small one.

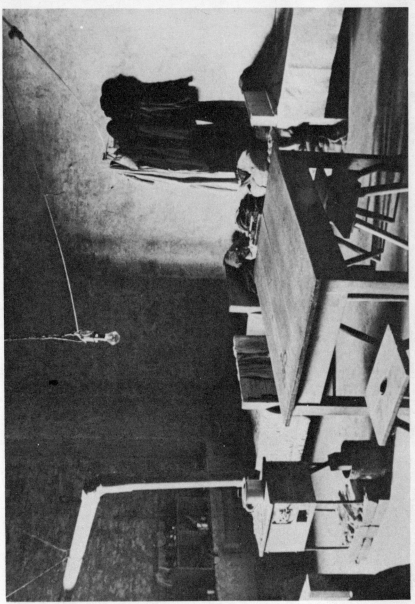

58. In an "emergency" building in Hamburg.

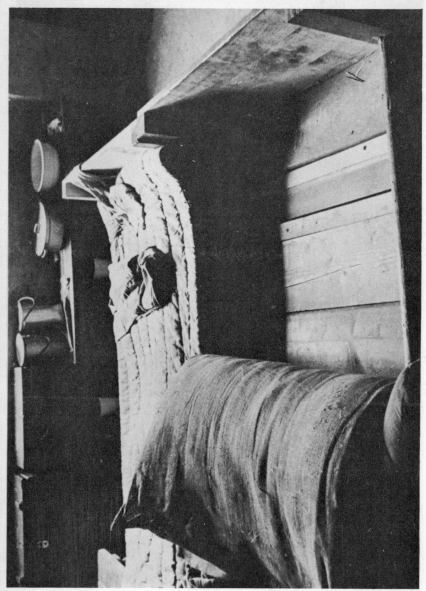

59. The same. One of the beds.

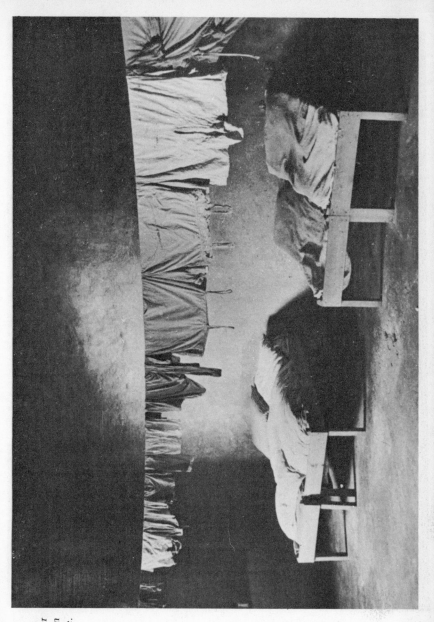

60. Another
room in
the same.

61. The
Gertigstrasse
bunker,
Hamburg.

62. The same.

63. The same.

64. *Nissen hut for prisoners of war in transit in the Stadtpark. Hamburg.*

65. Wooden hut in the Langenhorner Chaussee, Hamburg, housing eighteen people belonging to six different families.

66. The same.

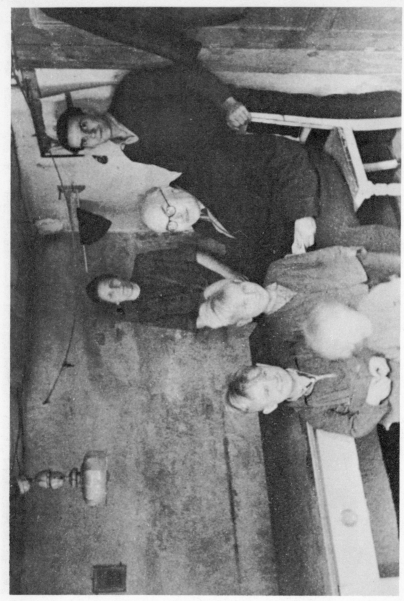

*67. Kleine
Marienstrasse.
Hamburg.
The sitting
room.*

68. The same. Ceiling of sitting room.

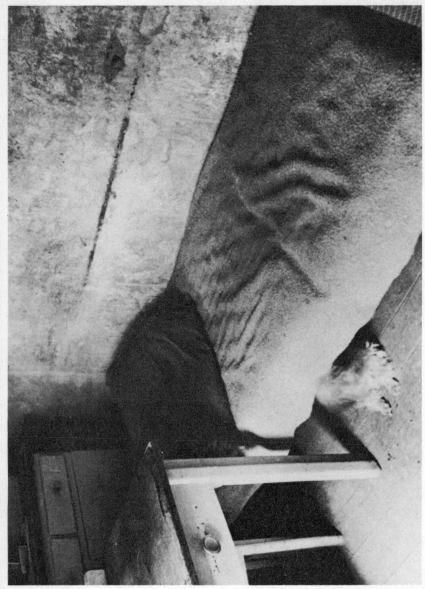

69. *The same. Bed in sitting room and dog.*

70. The same.
Mattress

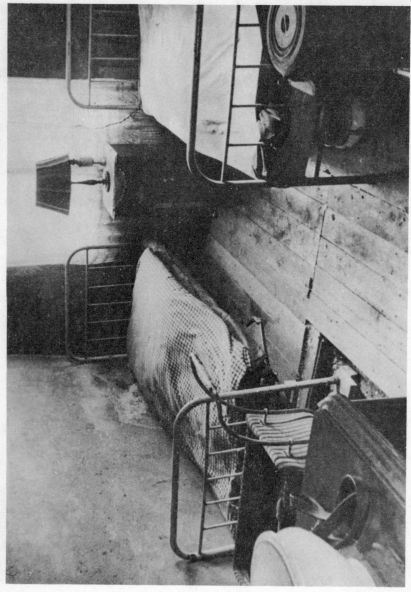

71. The same.
Bedroom.

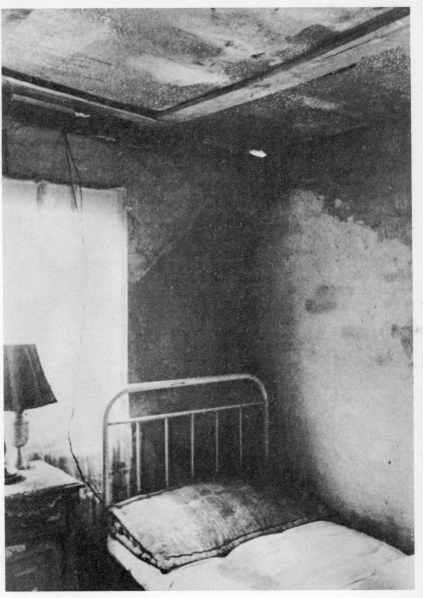

72 The same.
Wet pillow.

73. The same. Wet zinc ceiling of bedroom.

74. The same.
Outside.

143

75. The same. Another view.

76. "Geburts-
tag" room in
Lammstrasse,
Hamburg.

145

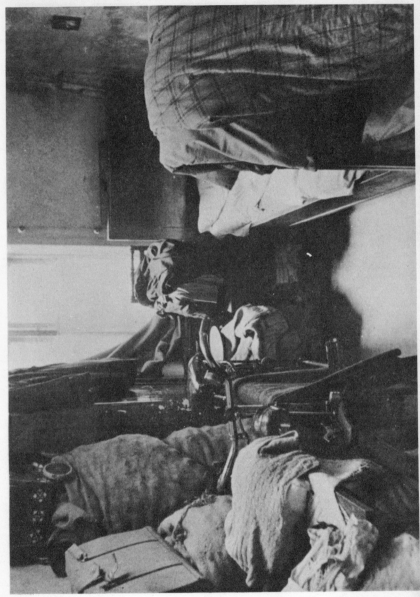

77. The
other room
in the
Lammstrasse.

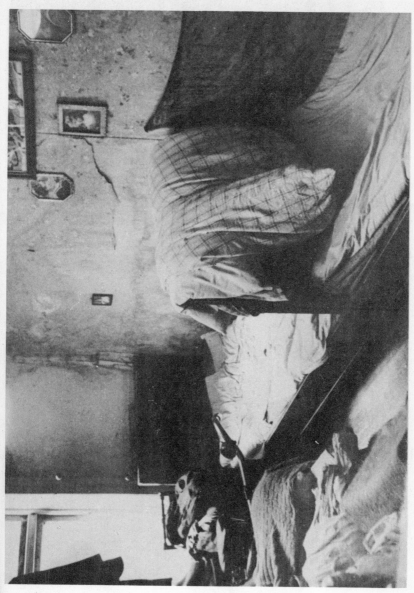

78. The same.

79. The kitchen in the Lammstrasse.

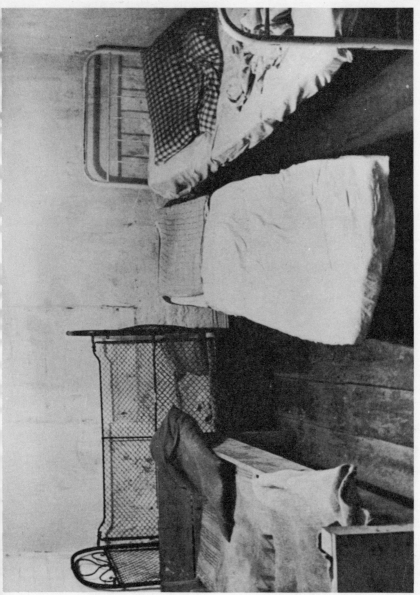

80. Cellar room with four beds (exceptionally) for four people, Hamburg. This was their only room.

149

81. The same. Entrance.

82. The flat where the communist lived. The bachelors' room.

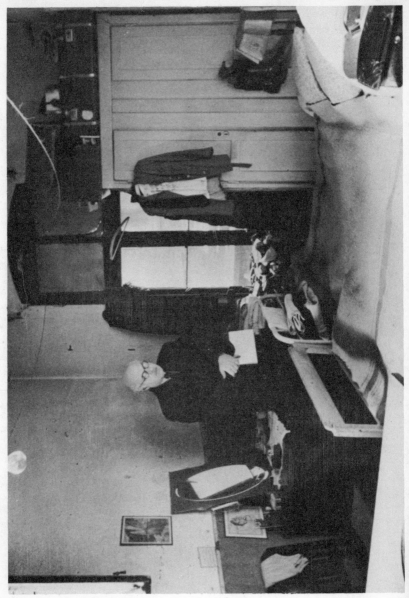

83. The same.
The room for
the five.

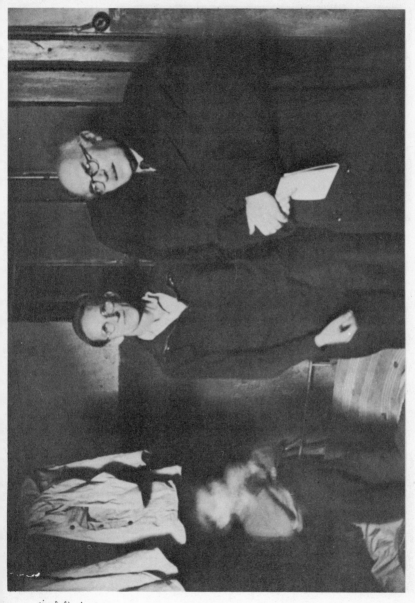

84. The same. The kitchen, with the communist.

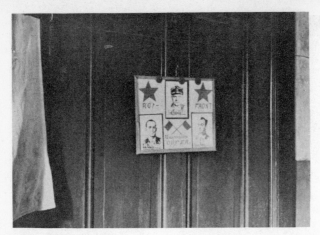

85. The same.

86. The same.
Down to the
lavatory.

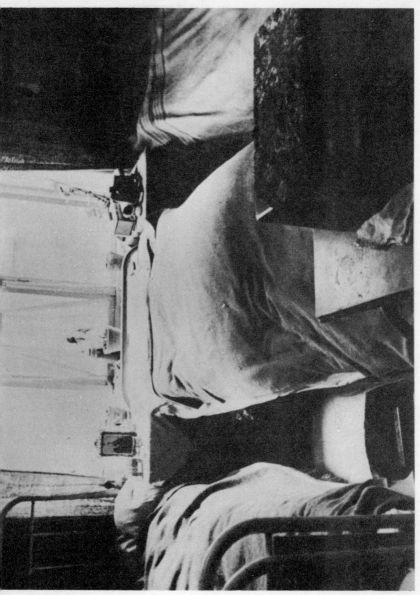

87. The room in the Repsoldstrasse, Hamburg.

88. The same.

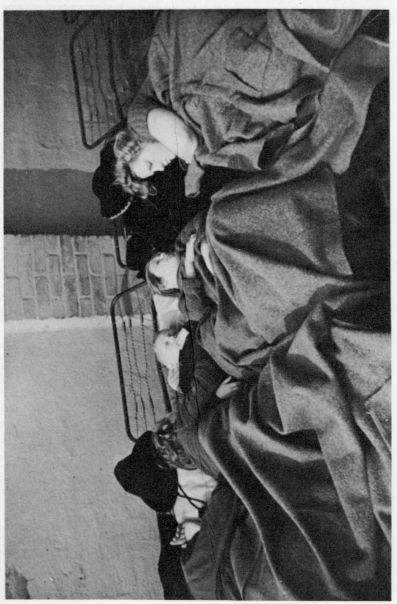

89. *Wanderers in the Jahnturnhalle, Hamburg.*

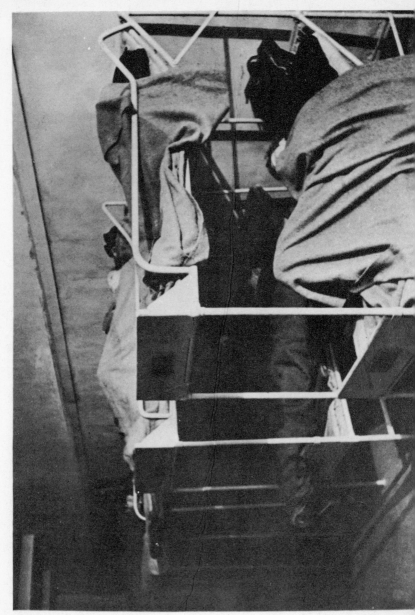

90. The
Asylum,
Hamburg.

91. Georg Böhlmann.

92. Düsseldorf. The mother who came back empty-handed.

Lerne leiden

ohne zu klagen.

94. Düsseldorf.
Nine
in one room
(one out).

95. *Miners' shacks at Oberhausen.*

96. The same.

97. *The worst shack I saw at Oberhausen.*

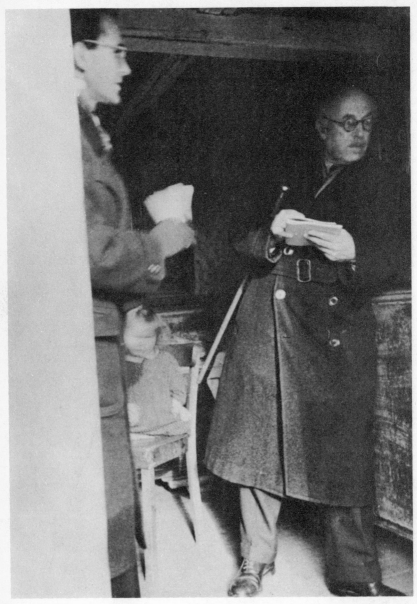

98. The same, living room. This photograph
gives you a good idea of the size.

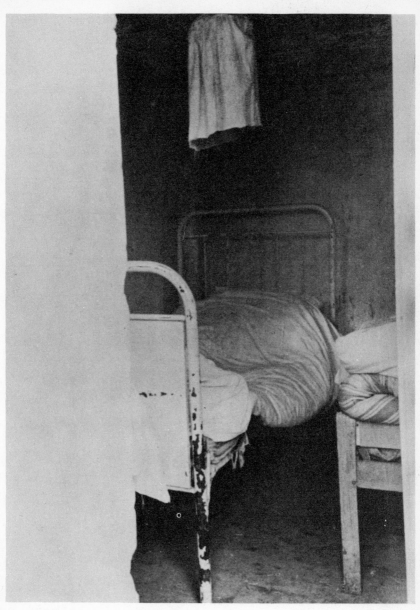

99. The same—one of the bedrooms.

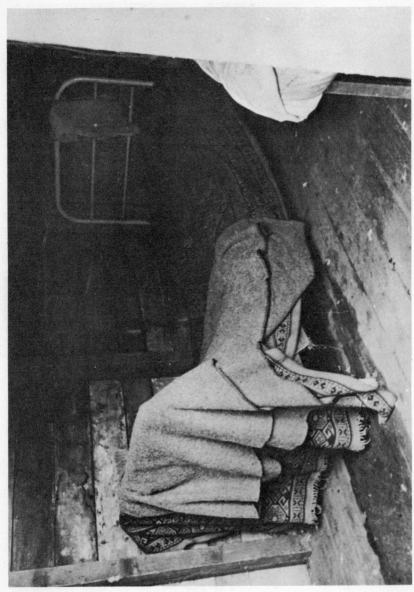

100. The same
—the other
bedroom.

101. *The same—some of the inmates.*

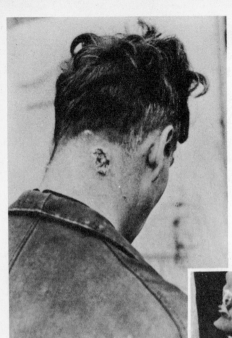

102. The same—the miner.

103. The same—the miner's son.

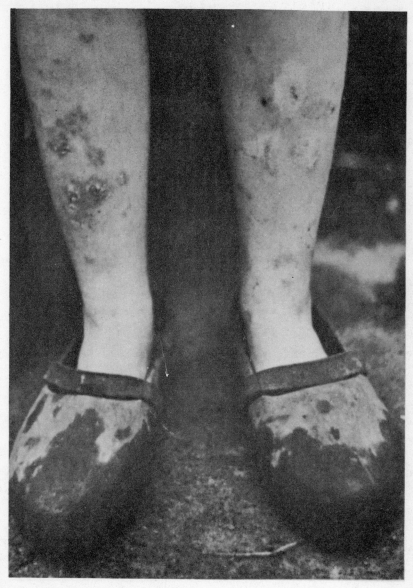

104. *Oberhausen. Sores and scars.*

105. Children in the camp at Oberhausen.

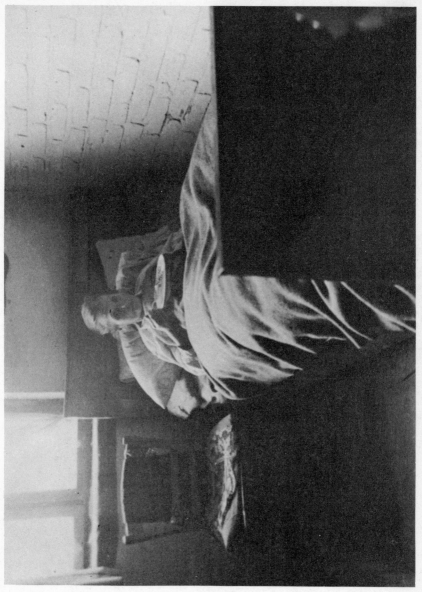

106. Oberhausen. The lady with asthma or heart trouble.

107. In an Aachen bunker. "In former days
anything so indecent would have been impossible."

IV

THE PLANNING OF RUIN

§ (i)

DORTMUND AND COLOGNE
(From the Daily Herald, Nov. 23)

I HAVE BEEN living for six weeks in a madhouse. I don't mean this metaphorically; I mean it literally. The world, unfortunately, has grown so used to being mad that it no longer notices its own condition. But as I drove through ruined Cologne at late dusk, with terror of the world and of men and of myself in my heart, for a moment I just couldn't believe that we were deliberately, eighteen months after the end of the war, adding further ruin to this unspeakable desolation. But that, and nothing else, is just what we are doing.

When Ernie Bevin made his anti-Potsdam speech in the House of Commons, it might reasonably have been thought that, pending developments, we would go slow on the reparations procedure. In my childishness I thought so myself. But not a bit of it: indeed, quite the reverse. Up till then, only four factories had been or were in process of being dismantled in North Rhine–Westphalia. Then at a Press conference on October 30th Mr. Asbury, the Regional Commissioner, thought fit to announce that "orders were awaited for dismantling" ten other factories, which he proceeded to name. He spoke, I understand, without the knowledge of Berlin; but there is nothing extraordinary about that, for in Germany nobody ever knows what anybody else is doing. Next day the German press added the names of two further firms. One at least of these had been officially notified by the responsible German body that it would be closed down very shortly: and the information "leaked".

Bear with me if I go into a little detail about two of these firms. The first is Hoesch of Dortmund. Now the life of Dortmund centres round three great concerns: and the more important part of one of them had already been closed down two or three weeks previously "on account of shortage of coal". The rumour spread that shortage of coal was all my eye and that the real reason was reparations. Mr. Asbury thereupon paid a special visit to the factory and assured the works committee that "the present decision to close the works was entirely due to shortage of coal. . . . No decision had as yet been made on the dismantling of the works for reparations." He spoke, I am sure, in good faith. But three weeks later came the press conference of October 30th. Asked at this whether it might be assumed that the factory would in due course reopen, a senior Düsseldorf official, in Mr. Asbury's presence, replied that it would be very unwise to draw any such conclusion. The fact is, as everyone now knows, that this particular factory was chosen for closure, when the coal shortage broke, precisely because it was to be eliminated under the "concentration of industry" plan—which is inextricably mixed up with reparations.

If Hoesch now goes the way of Dortmund Union (and the plan, when I was in Düsseldorf, was to close it down, or begin to close it down, in January) Dortmund—let us be quite clear about it—is ruined. The finances of the city, which depend very largely on this greatest of its firms, will go to pot. The supply of fertiliser, so desperately needed to increase German food production, will at best be interrupted; for a subsidiary of Hoesch, conveniently placed for using the slag, is one of the biggest manufacturers of fertiliser in the British zone, and now it will have to get such slag as it can elsewhere. The local cement factory will be similarly threatened, and the railway and automobile works that use the Hoesch products will be gravely handicapped, at the very time when an improvement in communications is near the very top of priorities. But forget all about that, and consider for a moment only the human aspect. 30,000 souls will be affected. It will be impossible to reabsorb in suitable work more than say a third of the skilled men, many of whom are in the third generation of service to the firm. The rest will become, at best, a species of slum labour, and will add a further burden to the ruined finances of the city; many, after decades at the blast furnaces, will die off miserably. The fact that the firm has one of the finest pension schemes in existence, and that a part, if not all, of its benefits will be lost to the men flung out, would have been worthy of mention in a saner and more decent age.

And what could be madder or more wicked than to throw tens of thousands of men out of work here and elsewhere just in mid-winter and just in the districts suffering most from the food crisis? If it had to be done, mightn't a better moment have been found?

The second firm to which I want to refer is Mathes and Weber of Duisburg. This is one of the only two firms in the British zone manufacturing soda. I haven't the faintest idea why it is to be closed down, and I dare say that a rumour to the effect that one of our allies is financially interested in the rival concern is so much malicious gossip. But what I do know is that the Germans desperately need washing-powder: that you can't make washing-powder without soda: and that if Mathes and Weber goes, Henkel, the great soap firm, may have to go too. And I ask again whether this isn't madness or wickedness or both. I ought to add that when I was there our Chemical Branch, which is concerned about soap, was making the usual frantic effort to secure a last-minute reprieve.

Or listen to this. The total capacity of the cement works in the British zone is 7,717,000 tons. 25 of them, with a capacity of 3,726,000 tons, are on the reparations list. Orders have recently gone out to affix "Law 52" to these works—and this is often the first step in the process of closing down. I shall be told that you can make pill-boxes and Siegfried Lines out of cement. So you can; but you can also use it to rebuild Hamburg and Düsseldorf and Dortmund—and Cologne.

What sort of re-education is this that we are doing, with our mania for destruction? Is that the way to make men democrats? Worst of all is the horrible uncertainty. Every German knows that there are many hundreds of firms on the reparations list; but no German knows what will be the ultimate fate of his own. If we *must* behave like vandals, at any rate let us publish a final list of the loot and then have done.

I hate fascism from the bottom of my heart. From the day Hitler came to power I thought of nothing from morning till night but how to prevent him and his accomplices and dupes from having their evil way. But I say that if now we choose the path of destruction rather than of reconstruction: if we fill the German people with despair rather than with hope: if we make them hate and despise us, when they were ready for emotions of a very different kind—then the Nazis, in spite of everything, have won, and tomorrow's world will be of their pattern and not of ours.

§ (ii)

THE LARGER AND THE SMALLER LUNACY
(From the New Statesman, Dec. 7)

It is difficult to write about German industry without making oneself look like a fool. The muddle and irrationality are so unbelievable that any attempt at describing them must invite the retort "But of course there's some good reason that you just don't happen to understand". I can only say that repeatedly during my visit I tried to get explanations, but almost always with a complete lack of success. No one knew more than his own bit of the story: and when after weary journeys from place to place you pieced the various bits together, they just didn't make sense. For all that, I think I know the explanation.

First, it is to be found in the way in which the whole thing has developed from the earliest days, if developed is the just word. When we first went in, this or that concern was "reactivated" at various levels, and often at the very lowest, to meet the immediate situation. I should judge that the Army did a first-rate job in those early months. But what was a virtue in the summer of 1945 became criminal lunacy when it persisted indefinitely: and things went from bad to worse when soldiers, acting *ad hoc* with the speed of a military operation, were gradually replaced by a vast and unco-ordinated bureaucratic machine, with no real change in the basic system. The superimposition of some attempt at planning, on a mere quarterly basis, has affected the all-over position very little. What has been totally lacking has been a strong controlling hand, which many months ago should have substituted for a chaotic series of spasms at the various levels a planned direction from the top: and a planned direction based, not only on a view that could look beyond next week, but on broad consumer needs (in which I include the need for producer goods) rather than on the competing demands of local producers. Moreover organisation, such as it is, has taken the form of parallel Branches that rarely meet. The coal and steel controls only slightly modify this picture.

The second explanation is, of course, Potsdam. There is an intellectual beauty about the completeness of the vacuum which separates zonal desires and necessities on the one hand from the impersonal operation of the reparations machine, positive and negative, on the other.

Æons, as it seems, ago there was some connection between the two: for the whole thing started with a tentative list of "war potential" and "surplus" firms and factories put up by the zone. That list has now acquired an independent robot's existence: bit by bit, in the form of embargoes on reactivation, orders to affix Law 52, visits by inventory-making commissions, and actual blowings-up and dis-mantlings, it comes crashing like some great stupid steam-roller into the zone (where meanwhile what Ibsen called "the local situation" changes monthly), creating un-certainty, confusion and terror. Branches and Divisions which suddenly see their plans, or their apology for plans, imminently menaced make frantic efforts to stay the monster's course: but usually in vain. This is no doubt an over-simplified picture. The list is modified from time to time: there are postponements, last-minute reprieves and so on: but by and large the picture is accurate. After a spate this autumn of placardings and inspections for reparation purposes, as well as of official threats, the position is at the moment obscure: the *Times* correspondent reported from Berlin on November 28 an official statement that "there will not be any further closing of iron and steel plants [these alone are mentioned] until at least the end of this year. . . . The statement contradicts the more optimistic reports that there would be no further closures this winter."

Let me give some examples of the lunacy that results from the operation of these two factors, and let me begin with the comparatively trivial and end with matters of life and death. I shall make no attempt to keep the one type of muddle distinct from the other: it would, indeed, be impossible to do so, for they are inextricably mixed up. And I am using only a tiny percentage of the material available.

For instance: (*a*) A blanket-making firm was allocated coal—but no power to run its machines. (*b*) A pin and needle factory was allowed to restart—but not to use its stock of raw materials, without which it could do nothing. (c) The Deutsche Delta Metall Gesellschaft of Düsseldorf has been refused a licence. Its products are needed by other metal industries. Duly licensed firms, therefore, cannot carry out their planned production. (d) A firm in North Rhine-Westphalia urgently needed a small quantity of building materials for indispensable repairs. It was granted them, but with the proviso that they must be obtained outside the city. You have to get a special permit to take a lorry more than 80 kilometres from its place of residence. This permit was refused. (e) The only Düsseldorf concern able to repair street cars was given a licence to operate that particular department. The licence was withdrawn without reason given, and the installation and personnel have been idle for months. (f) In the same city, Military Government recently ordered a drilling machine firm to vacate its premises within ten days. The effect on several industries (machine tools, optics, railway building, etc.) must be disastrous. The rumour was that a printing works was to be established on the site. But there is an idle printing works only 2 kilometres away.

There is a firm in Wesseling called the Union Rheinische Kraftstoff A.G. Its product is synthetic fuel. It could resume the production of petrol immediately, so that imports, which are at present 80% of consumption, could be reduced or even perhaps eventually discontinued. The raw material is brown coal from neighbouring Cologne, and the percentage used, relatively to the product, is very small. But all attempts to get a permit have failed. The reason: Potsdam prohibits the manufacture of synthetic fuel. Meanwhile, or so I am told, cars in our zone are being driven on synthetic fuel from Leuna, in the Russian zone.

It is proposed to destroy the quays and deep-water berths of Kiel harbour. If this is done, not only will Kiel

cease, as it should cease, to be a naval base: it will cease
to be a harbour at all, and no ships of any size will be able
to call there. Now the Kiel authorities, with commendable
pluck, are planning to build up a whole series of light
industries: but they are badly placed geographically, and
will certainly fail if their harbour, which is the natural
outlet, is lost to them. The highest British authorities put
the resultant unemployment at 150,000 out of a total
population of 250,000. The reason, again, is Potsdam.
But I have excellent authority for saying that the Russians,
far from destroying, are improving the harbours in their
zone—which marches with Schleswig-Holstein.

Even worse is the imminent plight of Hamburg. There
are, or were, three great ship-building works in the
harbour—Bloehm & Voss, Howaldt and Deutsche Werft.
Most of Bloehm & Voss has already been blown up—not
merely dismantled so that the material might be used
elsewhere, but dynamited into a mass of shapeless metal
that oppresses the mind with a sense of darker obscenity
even than the dust of Cologne, which at least was annihi-
lated, one remembers, under stress of war. Before the
dynamiting an attempt was made, from our side, to save
some very beautiful overhead cranes and electric motors:
really, it was asked, couldn't they be taken down and sent
perhaps to England? There was a moment's hesitation,
and then—"Blow 'em up!" (Plates 108–111.)

But four or five Bloehm & Voss installations nevertheless remain—among them a turbine repair shop, a sawmill, some small floating docks and a few exquisite cranes.
The turbine repair shop is the only one in Hamburg (and,
I rather think, in the whole British zone) capable of
repairing Hamburg's turbines, which are rapidly getting
worn out. The sawmill is of the utmost importance for the
rehabilitation of the port, as the other sawmills in the
neighbourhood of Hamburg are already overtaxed, and
sawmills are a bottleneck anyhow. The floating docks are

invaluable for the repair of ships up to 15,000 tons. The cranes, among the comparatively few surviving from the war havoc, are badly wanted for handling goods. Nevertheless the arrangement was that every square inch of Blohm & Voss was to be blown up, dismantled or sunk by the end of this year. When I was in Hamburg, some of our own people were trying their human best to prevent the reparations monster from crashing on. But I doubt whether they have succeeded: for the day I left Bünde for the Dutch frontier I received a note from a high authority giving "a list of factories which have now come into the category of 'condemned without hope of reprieve': these will be allocated and dismantled in the immediate future". There, at the top of the list, were four Blohm & Voss installations. I suppose at some time or other I shall have the heart to enquire whether they include the turbine repair shop and the sawmill and the floating docks.*

Howaldt was scheduled to be blown up or dismantled after Blohm & Voss: but it is at the moment intact, and as you come upon it in your launch after leaving Blohm & Voss it seems to have the grace of a living thing. Deutsche Werft is also said to be condemned. If these go, the port of Hamburg will be done for, as all facilities for repairing as well as for building ships will be at an end, and the place will be shunned. (Plate 112.)

While on the subject of ships I may as well give three examples of the minor lunacy. Item one. There were thirteen fishing vessels at Bremerhaven which were of the size permitted by Potsdam: but unfortunately they had been used as minelayers. The Germans proposed to reconvert them into fishing vessels. But no: we preferred to sink them or purloin them, or whatever it may have been, instead. Item two. There was a fishing boat a metre longer than the permitted size. The Germans wished to

* My fears appear to have been justified. See Appendix for Mr. Hynd's reply to a question on this subject.

lop off the offending inches—they put it in writing. But we blew the boat up—not once but twice, for the first time we didn't succeed—before the very eyes of the Hamburgers, and just at a moment when a food crisis was at its height. "The people say" added Petersen, the still friendly Burgomaster who told me the story, " 'The sea's full of fish, but they want to starve us.' " Item three. Some four months ago a licence was granted at quadri-partite level to build a hundred trawlers, in order to increase facilities for the landing of fish. Then an argument started about size. The Control Commission stipulated for 350 tons: the Germans pleaded for 500, pointing out that the smaller sort would be grossly uneconomical (the holds would be too small), and would be able to fish only within a narrow radius, whereas the larger could go to Iceland. The C.C.G. objected that trawlers of 500 tons might be used as minesweepers, and were therefore war potential. The dispute was still going on when I left Hamburg. Meanwhile, the wretched German fish ration has been reduced, and we complain that the cost of feeding Germany is almost more than we can bear.

I shall be asked, I suppose, whether I forget the horrible engines of war that Blohm & Voss produced. No, I don't forget them: I did my miserable best to warn people about them long before 1939, at a time when others who are now so tough about "the Germans" had a much better stomach for Hitler and Goering than I ever had. But I say that if there is one absolutely certain way of making a repetition of the last few years inevitable, it is to acquiesce in this godless destruction, and to drive a whole people, with whom somehow we have to live, into hatred and despair.

108. Blohm & Voss.

109. The
same.

110. The same.

111. The same—the remaining cranes.

188

112. *Howaldt.*

V

THE RE-EDUCATION OF GERMANY

§ (i)

HERRENVOLK

(From The Manchester Guardian, Dec. 2)

I was not surprised during my visit by the *Herrenvolk*
atmosphere, in which you gasp and stifle if you happen to
have been brought up as a liberal. The general standard
of honour, devotion to duty and even ability in the Control Commission is higher than rumour had led me to
expect; but the number of people I met who behaved in a
civilized fashion to the Germans—who mixed often and
freely with them, and treated them quite naturally as
equal human beings—was inconsiderable. I didn't, unfortunately, come into contact with many "other ranks",
and it may be that had I done so my all-over impression
would have been different. But the majority of officers and
civilians of officer status, or so I should judge, have practically no dealings at all with German males, except of a
purely official kind; and this is not, on the whole, from
"bloody-mindedness", but simply because that's the
atmosphere—that's the way ordinary daily life in an
occupied country works out, unless a special and continuous effort is made from the top to produce a different
situation. Though there are many very fine exceptions,
the general attitude varies from a disgusting offensiveness,
through indifference often identifiable with oblivion, to
that humane and almost unconsciously superior pater-
nalism which is characteristic of the "white" attitude to

"natives" at its best, or was when I was in Singapore in 1918. The indifferent and the paternal are far commoner than the disgusting, and it was perhaps unfortunate that I should have come across a specimen of the latter almost immediately after my arrival, and then another a day or so later. We were dining, not inadequately, at a comfortable mess; and there, in the presence of the German servants, a person of some importance in the establishment thought fit to say, and to say *à haute voix*, "I wouldn't dream of shaking hands with *any* German". Such blatancy is comparatively rare; but a more discreet discussion of Germans and their sins, while Germans handed the dishes, was by no means infrequent at messes at which I stayed or dined.

Here, as an example of something less crude but perhaps even more poisonous in its cold officialism, is an order that came out when I was in Hamburg: "Instructions in respect of German civilians attending cinema performances are cancelled, and a new procedure will be adopted. . . . Under the revised system . . . German civilians may only attend performances as guests of British personnel. . . . Presence of German guests will NOT, in any circumstances, be allowed to exclude British personnel and their families. . . . There will be two queues at each cinema: (i) one for British and Allied Officers and those of Officer status—no German civilians will be allowed in this queue; (ii) one for British and Allied 'other rank' personnel and German civilian guests." So if, you see, a British officer took the Burgomaster of Hamburg to a cinema, they would have to stand in separate queues— the host with the British officers and the guest with the tommies. In that order you have the present phase of the British occupation in a nutshell: the Germans are no longer pariahs, but they mustn't inconvenience the British and must keep their place.

In a certain city there is a certain hairdresser. Shortly after the capitulation four cubicles were set aside for

British officers and eight for Germans. No German was allowed to occupy one of the special British cubicles. This hairdresser recently became very popular with B.A.O.R. wives. One day a British lady had to wait some twenty minutes before she could get attention. Next day a major and captain visited the establishment, and told the proprietor that if a British lady were kept waiting again he would have his premises requisitioned. This alarmed the hairdresser, and a German lady was told to leave a cubicle in the middle of her hair-do. Then a very exalted personage took a hand, and the present arrangement is that four cubicles are set aside for British officers (male), four for British wives, and four for Germans. No German may enter any of the eight cubicles set aside for non-German personnel. The hairdresser is a very nervous individual, and rather than lose his shop he even today "requests" a German to leave one of the four cubicles when a British lady appears.

Though there has recently been a loosening of the restrictions on social contacts, and even some encouragement of them from the highest quarters, it is still extremely difficult for an Englishman of officer type to meet a German, except at rare intervals, on terms of normal equality. Before going to Hamburg I made some enquiries of a charming brigadier. I wanted to have a talk immediately after my arrival, I said, with a very distinguished German in that city, but not in his office: might I ask him to dine with me at the Atlantic? The answer was a very emphatic no. Might I then perhaps entertain him in my bedroom? No. What you had better do, he said, is to see whether you can get Mil. Gov. to put a room at your disposal at H.Q.—and, if you don't want it too formal, he added with genuine kindliness, have a few drinks! I am glad I took the precaution of enquiring, because a few days previously a German journalist who had been invited by, I think, a Swedish confrère to meet him at the Atlantic had been pounced on in the vestibule, asked "Are you a German?", and quickly hustled out when he confessed that yes, he was. Incidentally, he had spent some years in a concentration camp.

You may now ask a German to a meal at your mess if you get the approval, and ask him in the name, of the mess as a while. But though I was in Germany for six weeks, and stayed at messes nearly all the time, I saw no single German at any one of them. My own experience in this matter was peculiarly unfortunate. Having given due notice and received the necessary permission, I invited to dine with me, at what is officially a Headquarters Mess but really a hotel *de grand luxe*, a brilliant young German of my acquaintance. By a horrible mischance his British chief was dining at the next table. Later on in the evening I felt a certain strain, and noticed a look of blank fury on the face of my charming, humane and highly competent conducting officer, who happened to be an Irishman. It appeared that one of the colonels had sent for him, rated him soundly (in ignorance, apparently, that all formalities had been complied with), and threatened to have me removed, on the technical ground that visits at that particular mess were limited to a week. My Irishman threw his weight about, and interspersed his remarks with the names of Mr. Hynd, Sir Sholto Douglas, Mr. Attlee—and, for all I know, though he didn't dare own up to this, His Majesty the King. The upshot was that the courteous President of the Mess Committee told me how honoured they were by my presence, and begged me to stay as long as it might suit me.

In another city, three young Control Commission officers who were being transferred elsewhere wished to take a farewell meal at the house of a very distinguished German who was head of the "parallel" German organisation. They asked permission: this was first given, but next day peremptorily withdrawn. So they gave up the idea of a meal, and just went to say good-bye instead. They were severely reprimanded for doing so.

The plain fact is that there are two worlds in Germany today, the world of the conquered and the world of the conquerors. They meet at the peripheries, but their hearts beat in an inhuman isolation. I was talking to a high British official in Hamburg one evening: I had seen a man dying that morning at the hospital, had spent the afternoon in cellars where tens of thousands of Hamburgers live, and not yet being adequately hardened looked, I suppose, a trifle shaken. He asked me what was the matter, and I told him. "I wouldn't know anything about that" he replied, quite sympathetically. "I come to my office in the morning, do a hard day's work, and then go back to the mess and relax. For knowing anything about the life of the Hamburgers I might just as well be in Whitehall."

I was not surprised by any of this, as I said at the beginning, because previous visitors had warned me of what I might expect. But I wondered, and I wonder still, whether the best way to "re-educate" people cursed by a *Herrenvolk* tradition is to behave like *Herrenvolk*—if in the main very kind and decent *Herrenvolk*—yourselves.

§ (ii)

TOTALITARIAN DEMOCRACY
(*From The Manchester Guardian, Dec.* 3)

And the same might be said about militarism. Wherever you go in Germany the military character of the occupation stares you in the face. Enormous posters—"To the Yacht Club", "To the Officers' Club", "To Guards H.Q.", "Entry Strictly Forbidden to Civilians [*i.e.*, Germans]"—you are assaulted by them everywhere. You go into an office, and one of the first things you are likely to see is "This lavatory reserved for British personnel". The huge Victory Club in Hamburg, which might house thousands of cellar-dwelling Germans, blazes away by night in the ruined and darkened city. Naafi gift-shops and the like, which are no doubt necessary, are sometimes to be seen flaunting themselves with crammed shop-windows on conspicuous streets—not from any calculated cruelty, but because psychological reactions are ignored or more commonly just overlooked. The result of it all is that when German liberals talk to German youth about German militarism, the reply is—I've been told it again and again—"But British militarism is just as bad."

There is something graver, however, than these militaristic indiscretions, or even than our *Herrenvolk* superiority. Whether under Nazi or Soviet influence—and no one would underestimate the difficulties inherent in the quadripartite complication—we are behaving as if you could make men democrats by penalising them for their opinions, shackling their freedom of expression, and ticketing a vast section of the population into black (as *we* see it), very dark (ditto), rather dark, grey and white. In other words, we are trying to impose a formalistic democracy by totalitarian methods. You just can't do it. You can create democracy only by creating the conditions for democracy; if men are to have the chance of becoming democrats, they must breathe the spacious air of personal freedom and intellectual responsibility. There is simply no other way. I know very well the arguments on the other side: if people read "bad" books their minds will be poisoned; if the grey or even the half-grey are left without tabs on them they may intrigue underground; and so on. I reply—and what have we come to, that I should have to reply at all?—that if you censor a man's reading you make him a slave, and therefore excellent raw-material for the first shoddy fanatic that may be out to manipulate him; and if you forbid a man any decent employment and deprive him of his pension it isn't very likely that he will become a useful and contented member of society. Of course, there's a risk both ways; but in the one case you're taking a risk with God and in the other case with the Devil.

I have space to deal only with two aspects of this matter. Books first. The book famine in Germany is horrible. It is said that if a bookseller showed in his window a book about some obscure Indochinese dialect (if there is such a thing) a queue would form up for it almost as long as the bread queues I saw in Düsseldorf. The libraries, booksellers, publishers have suffered a triple catastrophe. First they were "nazified"; that is to say, all books by "Marxists", Jews and anyone ideologically offensive to the régime were sent to the bonfire. Then they were bombed; and if you are in doubt about how many books may have survived go and have a look at what was once the city of Cologne, and you will have your answer. Finally we came along, we British, and proceeded to "denazify". This hideous word, which in its very syllables expresses a world of intellectual shame and a posthumous capitulation to Hitler, at first meant purging German society of Nazi influences; but now it is also used with *men* as its object— you "denazify" a man by giving him the sack and making him clear away rubble.

The "directive" under which we purged the public libraries, booksellers and publishers—and for all I know also such private libraries as survived, if any one had the time or taste for snooping about in them—required the removal of all literature which included Nazi propaganda, contributed to military training or education, or "contained propaganda directed against the United Nations". To say nothing about the first two clauses, the third is pure and shameless Hitlerism in reverse. How has it been carried into effect? Well, here is what we have done with the Hamburg Public Library. All books dealing even remotely with Indian nationalism have been removed— among them Romain Rolland's "Mahatma Gandhi" and

Tagore's "Nationalism". Stored away too, and ready for shipping out of the country, are Fülöp-Miller's famous "Mind and Face of Bolshevism": a book by Jack London of which the title escapes me, but something to do with slums: and, to round the whole thing off, Lenin's "Imperialism". I can't imagine why Hitler spared it, unless he already had his eye on August 1939; but I know very well why we have repaired his omission. In that not very attractively written masterpiece Lenin analyses British as well as German and every other sort of imperialism; so no German must be allowed to read it. As for the Russians, they have published a book of prohibited literature: it runs to 526 closely printed pages.*

Having so satisfactorily proved our zeal in prohibition, have we shown an equal enthusiasm for fostering "safe", "suitable" or "democratic" literature? By no means. For all the shortage here, our book riches are beyond the dreams of any German for many years to come. Now while we imported into Great Britain 200,000 tons of chemical pulp, the Control Commission had the greatest difficulty in getting, during the same period, 16,000 tons for Germany. The population of the British zone is half that of Great Britain; and a little extra chemical pulp would permit of considerably increased production of paper, without additional wood or coal. What then does all our talk of "re-education" amount to? When I was in Düsseldorf translations of only two English books had been published since victory in North Rhine–Westphalia, which carries half the population; and I didn't think much of the selection.

The "directive" that controls the output of current German literature, such as it is, is even more drastic than that by which the libraries were purged. No publisher may publish a book which "reflects adversely upon the Military Government or any of the Allied Powers or is calculated

* See Appendix.

to create dissension between the Allied Powers". A serious study of Potsdam by a German economist: an objective comparison of Soviet communism and Western democracy: a translation of Lord Beveridge's *Times* articles: a novel or play about the frustration of German youth —these are a few of the pamphlets or books the issue of which would be unthinkable. What it amounts to is a total ban on most of the topics of living interest. And that is what we call "re-education" and democracy.

I have left myself little space to deal with the "denazification" not of books but of men. Let me say only this. There have already been three "denazification" procedures; and now there is to be a fourth, under which not only anybody who in future may apply for a large variety of jobs, or may be denounced or reported, will be placed in one of five categories (with appropriate penalties in the case of four), but everyone who has already filled in a Fragebogen or questionnaire on a previous occasion will come up automatically for "categorisation". This will mean the re-examination of nearly a million and a half Fragebogen; and people previously "passed", and who therefore thought themselves safe, may now find themselves subjected to penalties and restrictions. The uncertainty will be horrible. The Fragebogen itself must be seen to be believed. There are 133 questions—and among them the following: "Have you any relatives who have held office . . . in any of the organisations listed from 41 to 95 above?" "List on a separate sheet the titles and publishers of any publications from 1923 to the present, which were written in whole or in part by you and all the public addresses made by you, giving subject, date and circulation or audience." "List all journeys . . . outside Germany . . . persons visited." The German wits add a final question: "Did you play with toy soldiers as a child? If so, what regiment?" *

* See Appendix.

I asked one of the highest authorities on this procedure how long the re-examination of the Fragebogen would take. "About two years" he said—"but of course" he added "the whole thing will be discontinued before then." Then why, in the name of the liberal tradition of which we were once so justly proud, don't we set an early term to this disgraceful nonsense immediately, and give Germany the one thing she above all must have if she is not to go down into the pit and drag us all down with her—a new start?

§ (iii)

A FURTHER NOTE ON HERRENVOLK

The disparity between British and German living conditions, to some extent inevitable, is far greater than it need be. While millions of Germans are living four, seven or nine to a hole, our officers' messes are at worst pleasantly comfortable, and such of the senior ones as I visited were, for the most part, quietly and discreetly luxurious. Every time I entered such a mess before dinner the atmosphere reminded me very vividly of Singapore in 1918: there was the same sense of happy relaxation, the same feeling that you belonged to a privileged caste, the same climate of dignified well-being. I am not suggesting that many of these people did not work extremely hard, nor that, except in one or two cases, there was anything in the nature of vulgar display. The whole thing was far too well-mannered for that.

After the preliminary drinks, one definitely "dined"; and though the amount of food in any one course was not excessive, the number of courses, so far as the senior messes were concerned, almost invariably was. Further on I reproduce some menus, and these are not exceptional: I just slipped a menu card from time to time into my pocket when I was able to do so without observation. Germans meanwhile were eating as I have described above.

Most of the finest buildings still standing in the various cities are used as British messes or clubs of one kind or another, when not in occupation as offices. Many of our higher officials live in considerable state. I visited three of the four Regional Commissioners and stayed with one of them: the more modest type of residence was a mansion, and the less modest a palace. I am not saying this by way of criticism of the Regional Commissioners, for at least one of them, I know, intensely disliked the pomp in which he lived, and was planning to use part of the enormous space for unhappy children: but however strongly they might disapprove, being a species of colonial governor they had to submit. You could see the same kind of establishment, I was told, often enough in Berlin, but I didn't go there and so cannot speak from personal observation.

It is awkward to criticise the hospitality which I almost invariably received, but I ought to mention that at one mess at which I stayed in a particularly ruined city my bedroom measured 720 square feet. It was admirably furnished with two beds, though I had no bed-fellow, and a private bathroom was attached. There was central heating, a continuous supply of hot water, and "every convenience". As I lay in bed one night I happened to read a memorandum prepared by Dr. Arnold, the able and humane Burgomaster of Düsseldorf, for the religious delegation that had just preceded me. "The population very much regrets to see" he wrote "that the constructing and repairing of buildings for entertainment purposes is carried out by the Occupation Forces on such a large scale as would even have been remarkable in pre-war Germany, and that building material and labour are being used for this purpose, which might be utilised for the building of dwellings. On the other hand it is planned to close down factories manufacturing cement and building materials." In this connection, I have already mentioned the Victory Club at Hamburg (Plate 113); it may be added, to give a little more precision, that the labour and materials employed on it could construct 1,500 dwelling units and house 6,000 persons. The total cost of the work, which started in November 1945, is estimated at 13,000,000 marks. 1,500 men and 35 contractors are already engaged on the enterprise, which is expected to require 350,000 bricks, 800 tons of cement, 260 tons of iron, and so on. These are the figures of the German housing authority, which also states that "the works comprise dining-rooms, shops, rooms for management, ball-rooms, dancing-clubs, play-rooms, reading-rooms, sports-amusement facilities, restaurants, lounges, rest-rooms, bath-rooms etc., including staircases and lifts. Instead of the former cinema and theatre-hall a big ball-room will be built."

Now it happens that in a finely planned working-class quarter of Hamburg not only are the roads and sewers intact (which is half the battle), but the outside walls of the magnificent blocks are quite undamaged. (Plates 114–116.) If labour were employed here speedily, part of the Hamburg population, and in particular people living in the cellars below, could be decently rehoused with great economy; if, however, the buildings remain open to the sky, they will rapidly disintegrate. But nothing is being done about it, while work on the Victory Club proceeds.

A good deal has been said about the Hamburg Project, but I find that most people don't know what it is. There are only three more or less undamaged areas in Hamburg, and one of them is away by the river. In the other two, which are known as Zone A and Zone B, a great body of Control Commission personnel from all over the zone is to be concentrated, with office accommodation in other parts of Hamburg. This will be, in other words, a sort of Garden City for the C.C.G. When I was there, a total force of 14,226 labourers was engaged on the Project, of whom approximately 3,500 were employed on rehousing Germans evicted, or to be evicted, because of it, and on providing alternative office accommodation. That gives you a net figure of more than 10,000 labourers, as against 1,700 employed on ordinary civilian repairs for the miserably housed Hamburgers.* Meanwhile, perhaps 17,000 Germans have been evicted from their homes in Hamburg for one reason or another. This is a German figure; the British put it lower.

Mr. Hynd's repeated statement that Germans are never evicted until suitable alternative accommodation has been found was furiously denied to me, not only by Germans, but also by the British housing officer in one of the most seriously affected centres. In Düsseldorf the average living space per person is 3·2 square metres: if on top of that you proceed to turn out a lot of Germans to house a few British, where could the Almighty Himself find "suitable alternative accommodation"? On the other side of the account, the evidence is indisputable that British accommodation— I am talking now of general living quarters, not of messes— is often absurdly lavish, not merely by comparison with German housing conditions, but absolutely. I have recently received from two different persons—one a Control Commission officer and the other a relief worker—a statement of the position in a small town, the population of which has been more than doubled by the influx of "expellees". 40 Britishers are living in 131 rooms from which Germans have been evicted, and 213 rooms in requisitioned boarding houses, containing 213 beds, are occupied by 69 Britishers, 5 offices, and a sergeants' mess. The occupants are partly C.C.G. personnel and partly "families".

In this connection, is it realised that when Germans are evicted they have to leave their furniture behind them, including beds but not, mercifully, bed-clothes? No single British action has caused such bitter hostility, for many of these people have been bombed out three or four times, and specially treasure what they have managed to save.

* See Appendix.

They are told that their things will be returned to them when the premises are derequisitioned. This is certainly the rule, though there have been scandalous breaches of it, at any rate temporarily; but it is cold comfort to be told that you will get your bed back one day when meanwhile it is virtually impossible to buy another. In spite of everything written in this book, I only once felt ashamed of being a British citizen; and that was when I was told about a German musician whose bed—let us call a spade a spade—had been stolen from him.

. . . . .

Every C.C.G. officer receives, as a matter of right, 200 cigarettes, a box of matches, a piece of soap and a fair amount of chocolate every week. The German ration of cigarettes is about seven a week, and they get once a month either a small tablet of "schwimm" soap that looks as if it would disappear after a couple of applications, or a piece of nondescript material, detestably hard, with which I found it impossible to wash at all. In addition, an Englishman could buy at the Atlantic a piece of soap every day, as well as towels and other similar articles of necessity or pleasure. I tested this out for myself. I was told that you could freely buy in the same way at country clubs and the like.

The wife of an education officer told me that though she and her husband shared everything equally with their two German servants they still had twice as much food as in England. I give this statement, which I did not attempt to corroborate, for what it is worth; but I can think of no reason why the lady should have wished to deceive me.

Food and drink are fantastically cheap. I lunched or dined at such places as the Atlantic at Hamburg and a club at Celle for about a third of what a similar meal would cost at home.

The fact is that life is far too easy for the Control Commission. I know that this will be furiously denied, and not least by some of the most humane men out there, whom I learned very greatly to respect: but that is because, in occupation conditions, many even of the best people have inevitably lost any vivid realisation of the contrast between their own conditions and those of the people among whom they live.

§ (iv)

SOME MENUS AT OFFICERS' MESSES

(The mistakes have been retained)

(1)

Consommé in cups
—
Fried Soles in butter
Fresh Potatoes
—
Dutch Steak
Mashed Potatoes
Cauliflower
—
Raspberry Cream
—
Cheese
—
Coffee
—
Tuesday, October 8, 1946

(2)

Hors d'oeuvres
—
Tomato Soup
—
Rumpsteak
Garnie
Chip Potatoes
—
Creamed Caramel
—

Cheese—Biscuits
—
Coffee
—
Friday, November 1,
1946

(3)

St. Germain Soup
—
Braised Beef
Cauliflower au Gratin
Fondant Potatoes
—
Apple Tart
Cream
—
Welsh Rarebit
—
Coffee
—
Saturday, November 2,
1946

(4)

Hors d'oeuvres
—
Consommé
—

203

Vienna Steak
Red Cabbage
Carrots
Castle Potatoes
—
Savorie
—
Cheese and Biscuits
—
Coffee
—
Sunday, November 3,
1946

(5)
Mockturtle Soup
—
Roast Pork
Brown Sauce
Stuffing
Beetroot Salad
—
Pears
Ice Cream
—

Cheese Straws
—
Coffee
—
Monday, November 4,
1946

(6)
Cream Soup
—
Vienna Steak
Curry Sauce
Peas
Salad
Sauté Potatoes
—
Liqueur Fruit Salad
—
Savorie
—
Cheese and Biscuits
—
Coffee
—
Sunday, November 10,
1946

113. The
Victory Club,
Hamburg.

114. *Buildings in Hamburg that could be salvaged.*

115. *The same.*

116. *The same. Inhabited cellars below.*

117. Hamburg. German News Service photograph.

118. The same. By my photographer, taken in July.

119. The
same.

120. The
same.

121. The same.

122. The same.

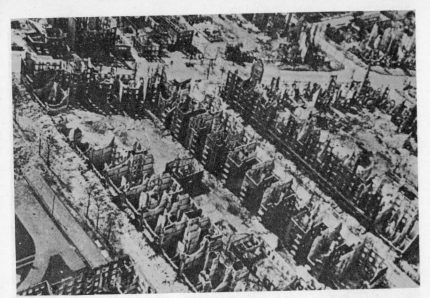

123. The
same.

124. The
same.

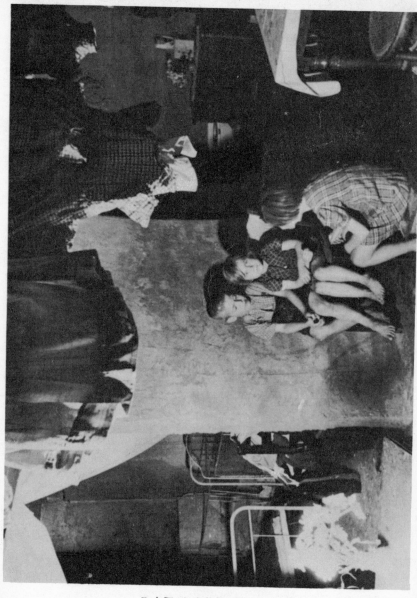

125. Ten people—mother and nine children, 4 to 19, live in this former air-raid shelter in Hamburg. No window. Entrance through long and pitch-dark stairway. Walls wet. No ventilation. German News Service photograph (July).

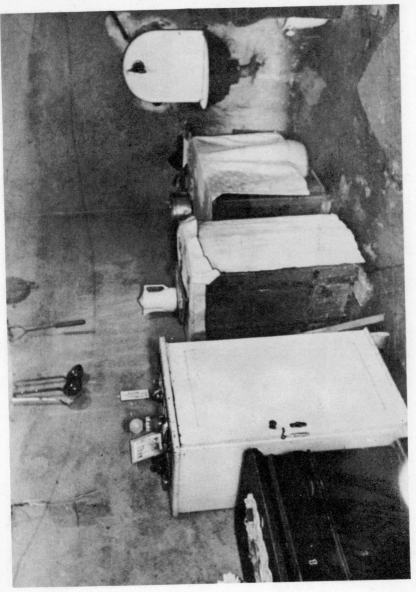

126. The
same.

127. Housing in Hamburg. German News Service
photograph.

128. Housing in Hamburg, German News Service
photograph, July.

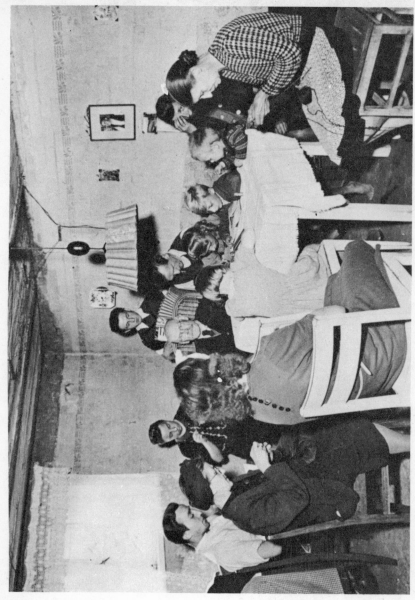

129. Hamburg. Three families in three cellar rooms, one very small. Taken by my photographer in July.

130. Hamburg. This was the basement by the canal which I visited with the Salvation Army people.

131. Hamburg. Inhabited by six people, including a baby. The room is wet. Salvation Army photograph.

132. Hamburg cellar. Two rooms, nine children, two grown-ups, five cups. Taken by my photographer, I think in July.

133. The same. Getting up.

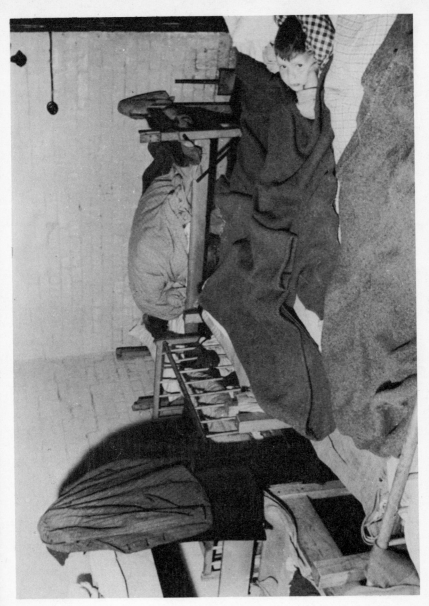

134. *The same.*

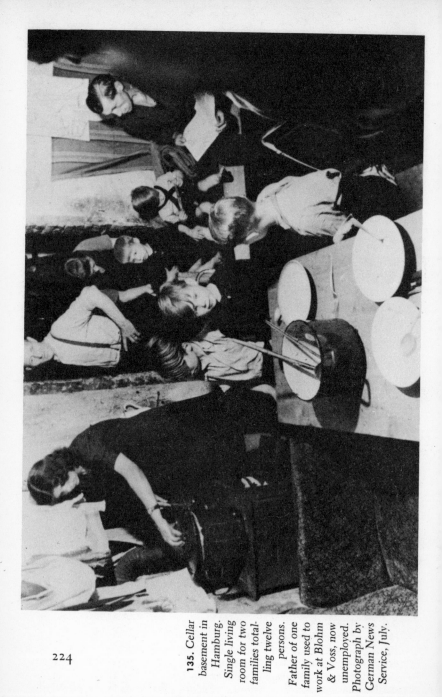

135. Cellar basement in Hamburg. Single living room for two families totalling twelve persons. Father of one family used to work at Blohm & Voss, now unemployed. Photograph by German News Service, July.

136. *Same cellar. Bedroom for one of the families.*
Just big enough for two beds. Sink used by other
family also. No window—small opening in nailed
door. Walls wet. Photograph by German News
Service, July.

137. The same. Lavatory three feet from bed.

VI

ISOLATION OF THE MIND

To the Editor of the Times Literary Supplement.

Sir,—There were times during my visit to Germany when I thought the intellectual and spiritual starvation to be even worse than the physical. Two or three weeks ago the Professor of Law in one of the great Universities took some of his precious law books to a friend who knew his way about the Black Market, and asked him to sell them for a pound of butter. His wife, he said, was desperately undernourished, and he had no further use for the books anyhow, as he was too feeble to read. Such tragedies are common enough, and by no means in Germany alone. But I met many young students who were quite resigned to physical hardship, but not to intellectual isolation.

I have dealt with the shortage of books, and particularly of English books, elsewhere. If a German happens to have a friend in Britain; if, further, he happens to know of the "Save Europe Now" parcels scheme, then he can cadge a book every now and again. I met, in point of fact, no single German who knew of this facility. But German after German, when they learned that I was a publisher, begged me to send them English books—this or that book if obtainable, but, if not, any books of any kind.

What applies to books applies also to newspapers and journals of every sort. De Crespigny, the Regional Commissioner for Schleswig-Holstein, told me when I was staying with him the other day that he receives in all 41 sets of English papers and periodicals for the whole of his region, the population of which is about 3,000,000. Until recently an ordinary German citizen was totally unable to obtain British newspapers or periodicals in any way whatever; now he can get them only if an English friend posts them out at his own expense. This closure on intellectual traffic is two-way. For a German to send German journals out of Germany is strictly prohibited. My friend Dr. Grimme, Minister of Education for Hanover, was good enough, two or three months ago, to write a little "piece" about me in a German newspaper. He enclosed the cutting in a letter. It was removed by the censor.

There is no greater danger in the Europe of to-day than this intellectual isolation of Germany, which is all the more disastrous as following 12 years of Hitlerism. I beg, therefore, (1) that visits should be arranged, on a really extensive scale, between the staffs and students of British and German schools and universities; (2) that parties of British youth should go out to Germany and live for two or three weeks with German youth on the German ration scale; (3) that parties of German youth should similarly be allowed to come to Britain; (4) that British universities should find out what books are urgently needed by German universities, should buy them by private subscription and should send them out through "Save Europe Now" or otherwise—I believe something of the kind already exists in embryo; (5) that everybody with a friend in Germany should send him good English books of any kind, asking him to pass them on if he doesn't want them; this may be done at the moment through "Save Europe Now", and perhaps by parcel post later on; (6) that the public should take full advantage of the little known Control Office scheme for the supply of books and periodicals to information centres and public libraries in the British zone: gifts for this purpose should be sent to Miss Goodwille, Room 12, Control Office for Austria and Germany,

Norfolk House, St. James's Square; (7) that writers, university people, and scientists should write regularly to their "opposite numbers", giving them some little information about developments here in an endeavour to mitigate their isolation.

Finally, I would urge—though I suppose this is hopeless —that when the time comes for our publishers' paper ration to be put up to 100 per cent. of pre-war, in the case of the larger publishers the extra percentage should go instead, for the time being, to Germany. There would be no material dividends; but there would be spiritual ones.

Yours, etc.

Victor Gollancz.

14, Henrietta Street, November 21st.

VII

GERMAN YOUTH

To the Editor of the Observer.

Sir,

The worst thing in Germany—worse than the malnutrition, the overcrowding, the gaping footwear in the schools—is the spiritual condition of the youth. I thought I had touched bottom in Jülich, where in cellar after cellar I found 5, 6, 9 people—fathers, mothers, children, adult daughters and sons—all jumbled together without light or air, and lacking even the pretence of any decent privacy. But a conference with young people at Düsseldorf a day later, and then another, were still more horrible; and what I learned then confirmed similar experiences with university students at Kiel and Hamburg.

The attitude of the youth varies from one of a puzzled bewilderment, still friendly to the British—these are in a minority—to bitterness, cynicism and a growing hostility to us and all our works. The mood is not (yet) pro-Nazi: it shows rather a nihilistic contempt for government and governments of every kind. They contrast our promises with our deeds: the B.B.C. told us, they say, that you were coming to liberate us, but what has it all amounted to? I mention democracy; and they ask whether democracy means starvation rations and lack of the barest necessities, or turning people out of their homes and seizing their furniture, or blowing up shipyards, closing down factories, and throwing tens of thousands of men out of employment. I risk a question about Nuremberg; and they say—at the very best—yes, they were guilty, but so are the Allies: look at the expellees, sick, starving and robbed, not thousands of them but millions. Many jeer openly at Nuremberg. I met no single young person who denied the Nazi guilt; but I met very few who thought it in any way special, or different in kind from that of all politicians everywhere. They talk a good deal about justice; and they want to know whether it is just to hale a man off to internment without trial and release him as innocent a year later. They talk, too, about their ostracism by the British on the one hand, and the behaviour of our troops to German girls on the other.

At the root is despair about the future. Time after time I was told "We don't mind how hard life is if only we can have something to hope for". But they see their factories being dismantled; they know that hundreds of other factories are on the list; and the majority are convinced that we are determined to ruin them, partly by way of punishment but mainly as commercial rivals. The minority wonders.

And yet—I am convinced of it after contact with them—they had, and perhaps still have, the makings in them of good democrats. After Belsen, the worst of all my experiences was when a university student at Hamburg said in an agonized voice "For God's sake don't make us Nazis". If we are to save them we must (1) stop doing the things they justly criticise, and give instead a living example of the liberal tradition; (2) put a little psychological understanding into our propaganda, which, on such subjects as war guilt or the world food situation, has been contemptible when it has not been non-existent; (3) increase the establishment of the education and youth section of the C.C.G., which is doing devoted work, but is as grotesquely understaffed as Trade and Industry is overstaffed, and is frustrated at every turn into the bargain; (4) remove the nightmare of uncertainty from the German future—which is to say, abandon Potsdam.

Yours, etc.,

VICTOR GOLLANCZ.

14 Henrietta Street, November 21.

138. Boy in an elementary school at Düsseldorf.

139. Boys in an elementary school at Düsseldorf.
Notice the bare feet.

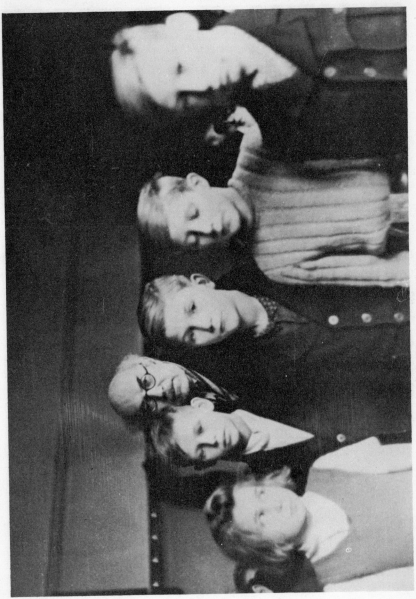

140. Children in another school in Düsseldorf. All looked ill, unhappy, and undernourished.

141. The
same.

142. Hamburg. Tripartite Nutrition Committee examining a school boy. Photograph by German News Service, August.

143. Boy in Hamburg searching for food in a garbage
tin. I should not have published this photograph
had not an education officer at Düsseldorf told me
that he saw the same thing himself while I was
in that city. German News Service.

144. Names on a door.

VIII

SUMMARY

(*From The New Statesman, November 30th*)

Mr. Hynd's recent speech in the House about Germany displayed a mixture of complacency and misinformation that is really beyond belief. This winter, he suggested, will be better than last. Of all the people I met during my six weeks' visit, I cannot think of a single one who would not laugh bitterly at such a suggestion. Here are a few of the reasons:

1. The Germans face this winter with physical and moral resistance lowered by a ration-card diet, for at least six months, of 1,000 calories. As everyone now knows, the recent "increase" was largely mythical. Perhaps 20 per cent. of the town population actually lives on this diet—and you can see what some of them look like in the hospitals and holes. The majority get just enough extra from the black market or otherwise to keep wretched body and despairing soul together. Apart from calories the diet, whether supplemented or not, is horribly deficient in fats and animal protein. The result has been a catastrophic increase during the year, in district after district, of all the evils associated with gross malnutrition—underweight, lassitude, hunger œdema and tuberculosis.

2. The appalling housing situation has been progressively worsened by the influx of vast numbers of "expellees"—and to a lesser extent by the incursion of B.A.O.R. wives and by such iniquities as the Hamburg Project.

3. People have been wearing out their last personal

and household possessions; and the supply of new articles to replace them has been hopelessly inadequate.

4. The commercial and industrial machine, such as it has been, is visibly running down. Coal is, of course, the crux. Mr. Hynd mentioned the recent increase in coal production; but he omitted to mention, not only that it was a "pick up" to only a little over the figure of output before the March ration cut, but also that the $6\frac{3}{4}$ million tons of coal and coke in stock at the end of the war were down to half a million tons by November, over and above an essential working reserve. Nor did he mention that raw steel production, which was 250,000 tons a month in August, was expected to be only 190,000 in October, on account of the coal cut. But shortage of coal is not the whole explanation. In addition (a) Stocks of all raw materials have become progressively exhausted. (b) Owing to this, as well as to the resulting necessity for inferior substitutes, the poor productivity of labour, the small percentage of capacity worked, and so on, it would be difficult enough to avoid huge losses even if there were a rational price and wages policy. But there is none: the general principle being to hold prices and wages at pre-occupation level, while discontinuing subsidies on the one hand and increasing working-class burdens by way of direct and indirect taxation on the other. The result is that business men must become hopelessly indebted to their banks, or sell their wares on the black market, or go slow in order to lose as little as possible. Many prefer the last. They keep their men nominally employed, but really hanging about day after day doing nothing. The amount of concealed unemployment is enormous. (c) Even such goods as are produced are to a large extent hidden, as producers, uncertain about the future of the currency and their own businesses, prefer goods to marks. Experts put this hoarding at as high as 50 per cent. (d) An indispensable condition, not for revival but for preventing a final break-

down, is a vigorous import–export programme. Nothing of the sort exists. I shall hardly be believed when I say that even to-day no German is allowed to send a business letter of any kind abroad.

The position in the early autumn was authoritatively summed up in the plain statement that trading had practically ceased.

I take the opportunity, as I pass these pages for press, to add some information that has become available since the above was written. Dr. Schumacher stated in London (*Manchester Guardian*, Dec. 3) that "last week, just before he left Germany, the cut of between 30 and 35 per cent. in industrial consumption of power (imposed at the beginning of October in North Rhine–Westphalia) had been increased to 60 per cent." And "Peregrine" reported to *The Observer* from Berlin on December 7 that "steel output is still decreasing".

5. The uncertainty of life—no one knows what may happen to him next week or month or year—grows increasingly desperate. There are two main causes. The first is Potsdam and the second is denazification.

6. As a result of all this and much more, we have lost—I pray for the time being only—the game of "re-education". In particular, we have all but lost the German youth.

What then to do? (1) Send a Resident Minister of Cabinet rank to the British zone. (2) Do at least what we can to ease the food situation at the cost of some national sacrifice. It is nonsense to say we can do nothing; I repeat, as one example, that if the Germans of our zone had been given the amount of meat by which our ration was increased a few months ago, they would thereby have received a regular additional 70 per cent. (3) Stop the export of coal for at least six months. (4) Unless we come to an agreement with Russia within a month, denounce Potsdam, and publish a final list of factories to be dismantled. (5) Put a term, and a very early one, to denazification. Find a policy which, without offending against the spirit of democracy and within the limits of democratic procedure, will (*a*) preserve acquired skills for German industry, (*b*) prevent men who think mainly in terms of private or national profit from getting a grip of the industrial machine, whether nationalised or not, and (*c*) give everyone, including those just mentioned, the chance of a decent and honourable livelihood. (6) Reform the financial structure without a moment's unnecessary delay. (7) Press on with a five-year plan for the rehabilitation of German industry, on the broad basis of public ownership and with a really adequate import–export programme. (8) Stop behaving like inefficient totalitarians, and try a little liberalism or Christianity instead.

Let me say again, to avoid misunderstanding, that while there are too many careless, stupid, unsuitable and perhaps not over-scrupulous men in the Control Commission, the proportion of personnel, both military and civilian, which reaches the finest possible standard of devotion, ability and honour is splendidly high. But these men, almost without exception, are frustrated by the unco-ordinated working of a bureaucratic machine, by the growing divorce between Berlin and the zone, and above all by the absence of a policy in London.

APPENDIX

"WHAT SAY THEY?"

Of the statements made in those parts of this book which have already appeared in the Press only one has been publicly challenged by Norfolk House. A week or so after the article "Totalitarian Democracy" (page 98) appeared in *The Manchester Guardian*, Mr. Houghton, Director of Information Services, wrote to that paper (December 12th) and attempted to controvert my remarks about the "denazification" of books. What he said in detail will be gathered from my reply (December 13th), which was as follows:

"Mr. Houghton's letter is another example of misinformation at Norfolk House. First, public libraries. On October 23 I interviewed the British official in charge of the Hamburg public library. He produced a very long duplicated list of the books removed before the present official's time. It contained those I mentioned. They were not 'segregated in the library' as Mr. Houghton suggests. They were in store at the offices of this official, and he produced those I wished to examine. Those 'wanted' abroad were presently, I believe, to be shipped out of the country. He further produced Control Council Order (May 13, 1946) under which this 'denazification' proceeds. It prohibits the circulation not merely of books 'supporting militarism, nationalism, and racialism' but— as Mr. Houghton omits, though it was the whole point of my article—books 'containing propaganda directed against the United Nations'. It is true that 'the responsibility for the complete handing over of the above mentioned literature rests with the holders as well as with burgo-masters and local authorities', but it is also true that 'control over the execution of the order will be exercised by the . . . representatives of the . . . occupying Powers'. My informant also said—I have a note made at the time—that 'the Regional Information Control Units (British) work within the Control Council order of May 13'. If Mr. Houghton thinks that, in view of all this, my sentence 'here is what we have done with the Hamburg public library' is incorrect, he is welcome to his point.

"In dealing with current literature Mr. Houghton confuses books, about which I was writing, with news-papers, about which I was not. The policy for newspapers is fairly liberal, though the very existence of the ban on certain types of criticism must have a paralysing effect, and the atmosphere can be gauged by the remark of one of our press officers to the effect that he saw German editors almost daily—'I go to them when it is nothing of real importance, and only summon them to me when it is'. But the book situation is very different. Every publisher receives a document of 'instructions', which informs him that the 'licensee is personally responsible that the works published under this licence shall not include anything which reflects adversely upon . . . any of the Allied Powers'. According to the same document, he may either submit a proposed publication for approval in writing, or may risk it and deliver to the book censorship bureau a first copy. After at last getting a licence (for which he has to fill up four questionnaires, containing in all 213 questions) how many publishers are going to risk losing it by publishing a book that 'reflects adversely on any of the Allied Powers'? I was indeed informed by a British official in charge of books that 'we encourage publishers to submit their books for censorship in proof form—because they won't go to the risk of setting the work up unless they are quite certain it is O.K.'.

"Let me put a plain question to Mr. Houghton. During the last few months would publication in German of a book exposing the idiocy of Potsdam or attacking Soviet Communism have been remotely possible?

"As to Lord Beveridge's 'Times' articles, if they were published in Hamburg in book or pamphlet form (it is this to which I was explicitly referring, and not to the press, which is allowed, by a general directive, to reproduce material from the British press), then of course I withdraw that particular instance. But I should be much surprised to hear that this was so. A young German was just about to get his publisher's licence when I was in Düsseldorf. He was anxious to start with a translation of the Beveridge articles. He told me he had made unofficial inquiries—as he had not yet received his licence that was all at the moment he could do—and had been informed that his proposal was out of the question. The one thing he now wanted to do was to get away from that stifling atmosphere and return to London.*

"If Mr. Houghton thinks I am wrong in describing all this as 'totalitarian democracy', that must be because he has forgotten, if he ever knew, what democracy means."

.   .   .   .   .

But while Mr. Houghton's letter has been the only direct challenge to my accuracy, several of Mr. Hynd's statements or replies to questions in the House have been out of harmony with what I learned on the spot. This discrepancy is mysterious, for presumably the people who brief Mr. Hynd in London get their information from

* On reading Mr. Houghton's letter I at once wrote to Hamburg. I receive a reply as I go to press. My informant, a C.C.G. official who is in a position to know, writes that he is unaware of any publication of the Beveridge articles in book or pamphlet form. He adds that the German News Service was at first not even allowed to circulate the articles for reproduction in the German press (in spite of the general directive which permits such reproduction) owing to a Norfolk House decision, but that subsequently this decision was reversed under pressure.

officials in Germany. I have no explanation to offer, but will give two examples:

(1) Replying to a question in the House on December 4th about the number of workers employed on the Hamburg Project and on the building and repair of houses in Hamburg for German civilians between October 20th and November 19th, Mr. Hynd said:

"There were on the average some 9,000 Germans and 180 British employed during this period on the Hamburg Project, and 1,400 Germans employed on emergency civilian repairs. The figure of 9,000 includes, however, some 2,500 engaged on rehousing for Germans and some 1,400 employed in providing alternative office accommodation for Germans. Some 5,100 Germans are, therefore, engaged on the Hamburg Project proper and 5,300 on accommodation for German civilians."

I have before me a document prepared in Hamburg during October by a responsible officer of our Manpower Division there, as the result of a request made by me to the head of Public Relations in that city. This shows 14,226 as the total force employed on the Hamburg Project, made up of 5,815 Hamburg men, 4,372 imported and living in camps, 853 imported daily travellers, and 3,186 Dienstgruppen (undemobilised soldiers used as building labourers). The document further shows that of this total approximately 3,500 were employed on rehousing Germans to be evicted on account of the Hamburg Project, and on providing alternative office accommodation. Mr. Hynd's figure of 1,400 Germans employed on ordinary civilian repairs agrees roughly with the one I was given.

We therefore get, instead of Mr. Hynd's "5,100 Germans employed on the Hamburg Project proper and 5,300 on accommodation for German civilians" (which would be disgraceful enough), a *net* force of over 10,000 employed on the Project, and 1,400 (or, to give my figure, 1,700) employed on ordinary civilian repairs.

Are we to understand that there was a sudden and very heavy reduction? But the same document says "at present 1,352 men are required"—i.e. in addition to those already employed.

(2) Mr. Hynd was asked by Mr. Skeffington-Lodge on December 11th whether all the questionnaires already filled in by the Germans for purposes of denazification were to be re-examined, with a view to placing all individuals concerned in one of five categories. His reply was that this was not the case, and that only 234,000, relating to persons who have been removed or excluded from office, were to be re-examined. This reply categorically contradicts a statement made to me at Bünde on November 12th by Brigadier Gaffney, to whom I had been referred by Public Relations for authoritative information, and who is deputy chief of denazification for the whole zone. The interview was not in any sense confidential, and I made detailed notes of what he said as I sat at his table. He told me quite definitely that all the 1,368,739 *Fragebogen* would be re-examined with a view to categorisation. I then specifically asked him whether that applied to people in jobs. He said that it did. I asked whether any of these people would be liable to penalties. He said that yes, they would be so liable if placed in any category other than 5 (the exonerated), but that people in jobs would presumably be categorised below category 3, and that therefore at worst only "minor" penalties would be applied to them. A reference to Control Council Directive No. 38 (signed on October 12th 1946 by, among others, General Erskine for General Sir Brian Robertson), on which the zonal instruction is to be based, shows that these "minor" penalties (for category 4, or "nominal" party members) may include periodical reportings to the police, withholding of permission to leave Germany or a particular zone, loss of the right to stand for election at any level, retirement of civil servants or transfer to an office with

lesser rank (and corresponding measures against persons in economic enterprises), and single or recurrent fines.

Unless, then, there has been a last-minute change, whether or not as a result of protests, either Mr. Hynd or the deputy chief of denazification is misinformed. Neither of these alternatives seems satisfactory.

. . . . .

In such cases there appears to be a direct conflict of evidence. Other statements carry on their surface, or a little below it, their own refutation. In answers to Parliamentary questions, for instance, it sometimes happens that part of the enquiry is ignored and the remainder "telescoped": the result being a false conclusion, which is the more to be regretted when it occurs in a written answer, and so cannot be challenged by supplementaries. Such cases are to be explained, no doubt, by ignorance of the points involved.

An example. On December 11th Mr. Michael Foot asked the Chancellor of the Duchy what quantity of bread the normal consumer in Düsseldorf should have received during the 28-day period starting 14th October in order to provide the quota necessary to make up 1,548 calories; what quantity of bread he was actually entitled to receive; and if there was sufficient bread to provide the *latter* quantity [my italics] or what was the deficiency. Mr. Hynd replied in a written answer:

> "The amount of bread necessary to make up the full ration was 10,000 grammes."

This is correct. He continued:

> "The limited supplies of grain available only permitted a ration of 8,500 grammes."

This is correct, if understood as replying to the second part of Mr. Foot's question, namely "what quantity of bread he was actually entitled to receive." Only 8,500 grammes were "called up"—i.e. no one was entitled to buy more than 8,500 grammes. But when Mr. Hynd concludes:

> "leaving a deficiency of 15 per cent."

he is wildly incorrect. For he has ignored the third part of the question, namely "and if there was sufficient bread to provide the latter quantity"—i.e. the 8,500 grammes. The fact is that during the first three weeks of the period there was sufficient bread to provide only about 50 per cent. of the "called up", the 8,500, ration. (I made my investigation during the fourth week, and so was able to get figures for the first three weeks only.) What people actually got to eat that month, therefore, was not 85 per cent. of 10,000 grammes but (on the unwarranted assumption that the 8,500 ration was met in full during the fourth week) say 60 per cent. of that 85 per cent. In other words, the total deficiency was not 15 per cent. but about 50 per cent. And remember, please, that we are not talking about trivialities; the difference between Mr. Hynd's figure and the real one is the difference between a little less bread on some days and no bread at all on many.

.　　.　　.　　.　　.

Of a different order are statements that are liable, but not of course designed, to mislead. Here, again, is an example:

Mr. Hynd said on November 27th that "we proceeded to dismantle, or to allow the dismantling of, seven plants. . . . Beyond that, we are not proceeding with any dismantling at the present time." A little earlier the Minister had qualified the figure seven by "I think". If challenged in a court of law this statement could be successfully defended even by inferior counsel; for indeed we are not at the moment actually removing anything from any factories other than the seven (which are incidentally nine) to which Mr. Hynd referred. But would a man be unduly innocent if he concluded from the Minister's statement that, for the time being at least, we were suspending the whole "procedure"? How many would be likely to infer that we have been meanwhile "proceeding" with the various steps that culminate in dismantling—affixing Law 52, inspecting, valuing, and finally allocating to one or other of the I don't know how many harpy-nations that have been hovering in Brussels for their share of the prey? Could M.P.s have expected that when, only a week later, Major Bruce was to ask whether it was proposed to dismantle the turbine repair shop or the sawmill or the remaining cranes at Bloehm & Voss, Mr. Hynd would reply that yes, they were "due to be dismantled and removed after allocation by the Inter-Allied Reparations Agency "? Was the Chancellor aware, to use the parliamentary formula, that, as stated in the text, I had received from the head of our Reparations Division in one of the most important *Länder*, and as lately as November 14th, the day I left for home, a list of "factories which have come into the category of 'Condemned and without hope of reprieve'. These will be allocated and dismantled in the immediate future"? Could anyone have imagined, as they heard the words "we are not proceeding with any dismantling", that, as also stated in the text, the Regional Commissioner of North Rhine–Westphalia had declared with the maximum of publicity—to be precise, at a press conference—exactly a month before that "he was awaiting orders for dismantling" certain factories, the names of which he gave and circulated? And finally, what reactions would be likely in Members who happened to hear a statement put out on December 3rd by the British-sponsored German News Service, as follows:

"Cologne: It was announced today at a press conference of the Cologne Chamber of Industry and Commerce that important machine-tool plants in the industrial area of Cologne are to be dismantled. The factories concerned are: Alfred H. Schuette A.G. at Koeln-Deutz, Hermann Kolb at Koeln-Ehrenfeld, Maier, Roth & Pastor A.G. at Koeln-Raderberg, Mueller & Schwamborn, Machine factory C.M.B.H. at Rodenkirchen.

"The Alfred H. Schuette A.G. was, apart from Pickler

in Leipzig, the only plant in Germany producing multi-spindle automats. It also manufactured precision parts for tool machines. Hermann Kolb is the only firm in the British zone producing a special kind of drilling machine since the Hetter tool machine factory in Muenster-Eifel was destroyed and also put on the dismantling list. The Maier, Roth and Pastor A.G. is producing chain-welding machines for the mining industry and also wire and masts. The Mueller & Schwamborn machine factory is the only firm in the British zone producing wire-rope machinery for the mining industry."

I am not suggesting for a moment that Mr. Hynd intended to mislead; what I do suggest is that, driven by his position to defend things of which all who know him must suspect he disapproves, he made a statement less open to criticism for the letter of it than for the spirit.

Is the reader convinced? If not, perhaps this extract from *The Times* will convince him. The date-line is Brussels, December 11th:

"The inter-allied Reparations Agency denies Press reports that no further industrial reparations will be forthcoming from the British zone of Germany.

"Arrangements have just been completed between the Commander-in-Chief of the British zone and the Agency for the *immediate* release, as reparations, of general purpose machine-tools and equipment to a value of 75,000,000 reichsmarks. The Agency expects that the allocations of this equipment among its 18 member-nations entitled to receive reparations from Germany will be completed *early next year*. This amount is *additional* to other plant and equipment in the British zone which has already been allocated by the Agency to member-nations and *will soon be dismantled and removed*."

The italics are mine.

THE END